WHISTLE THE WIND

Hardly a Scholar
(Second Edition Kennedy & Boyd 2009)
Ken Shearwood's vigorous and lively autobiography is the story of a successful life, way out of the schoolmaster's common run. Now in his eighties, Shearwood tells of his schooldays at Shrewsbury, of harrowing and hazardous times on destroyers and landing craft in the Second World War, a first career spent professionally inshore fishing off Cornwall, and then, admission to Oxford with about as few academic qualifications as one can reasonably imagine. No matter; an excellent all-round games player, and at soccer a frankly uncompromising centre half, Shearwood was to become an integral part of the briefly flowering Pegasus side from Oxford and Cambridge which, remarkably, twice won the Amateur Cup.

Colin Leach, Times Literary Supplement.

Pegasus
(Oxford Illustrated Press, 1975, Second Edition Kennedy & Boyd 2009)
Though the central theme is Pegasus, this is more than the mere history of an original football venture, offspring of Centaur and Falcon, which soared like a brilliant comet and died within a crowded decade and a half, victim of its own early success. Across these pages is woven a wider human pattern — esoteric days at Oxford, the trials of parenthood, cricket in high summer, the growing pains of a schoolmaster at Lancing.

Geoffrey Green, sport correspondent, The Times

Evening Star
(Bradford Barton, 1972)
A tale about Mevagissey during the 30s and, in particular, a Cornish lugger and her crew, which fished the waters from Wolf Rock to Start Point.

...a tale with immediacy and impact...   *The Cornishman*

Whistle The Wind

A Mevagissey Venture

Ken A. Shearwood, D.S.C.

Illustrated by
A.J.Ingram

Kennedy & Boyd

Kennedy & Boyd
an imprint of
Zeticula
57 St Vincent Crescent
Glasgow
G3 8NQ
Scotland

http://www.kennedyandboyd.co.uk
admin@kennedyandboyd.co.uk

First published by Rupert Hart-Davis in 1959.
This Edition published by Kennedy & Boyd 2009

ISBN-13 978 1 904999 17 1
ISBN-10   1 904999 17 4

TO MY WIFE
BIDDIE

Contents

CHAPTER ONE

The *Coral*

THE treacle tart lay broken on the floor. It is from such trivial incidents that much of the pattern of life stems, and this story, which began with a culinary failure on the part of my wife, resulted among other things in my becoming a fisherman, an undergraduate at Oxford and then a schoolmaster. It led also to my playing much football, including two Cup Finals at Wembley, and some cricket for the University. But that is all another story. First and foremost, the episode of the treacle tart led to my meeting with George Allen, the results of which were to help shape the course of my post-war life. It is with these results that this story is concerned, so it is right and proper to go back and start at the beginning.

It all began one cold evening at the end of January, 1946. My wife and I, attracted by the brightness and warmth of a cinema and to gain a brief respite from the bitter wind, ran up the steps, passed through the swing doors and, on the spur of the moment, decided to take a chance and see the film.

This decision was the first unconscious effort which resulted in my becoming, for a short time, an inshore fisherman. I suppose on reflection that we were irresponsible in our outlook on life, living and enjoying each moment instead of planning ahead and saving our money. But, if we had been people like that, events would never have fallen into this particular pattern. And we should have been the losers.

We had been recalled from our honeymoon in the wilds of Yorkshire, not highly successful, for we had both caught 'flu, in order to report to Lowestoft for demobilisation. All that day had been spent in going through the rather dreary routine of medicals and form-filling, waiting in queues and eventually selecting some suitable clothes for peace-time.

The cinema was warm, and the film, *Johnny Frenchman*, a most enjoyable one. When eventually we emerged into the cold night and walked back to our hotel the wind was blowing hard from the east and the noise of the sea sounded ominous and threatening.

I had spent the last four years at sea in destroyers and landing-craft. During my sixteen months on the lower deck in destroyers we had operated from Harwich, and I had a wholesome respect for these waters.

As we bent forward, leaning into the wind, I had no clear picture of what I was going to do. My total assets appeared to be some newly acquired clothes, about £900 and a sweet wife. I had done a year at Liverpool University, studying architecture, but somehow the thought of returning was not agreeable. Endless studies interspersed with frequent attempts to satisfy examiners were a gloomy prospect.

We hurried down the last draughty street to our hotel, anxious only to escape the cold.

Later as I lay in bed listening to the sound of the sea, my mind wandered back over the day's events, beginning with the final medical inspection and ending in the comfort of a cinema, watching the sure and easy acting of Françoise Rosay and the fine photography of a Cornish fishing village tucked between great flanking cliffs. Sea and wind, demobilisation, Liverpool University, peace: somewhere amid all this lay the dim future and among such thoughts, accompanied by the rattling of the window as great gusts of wind hit the panes, we drifted asleep.

Next day was fine, and after an excellent breakfast of fresh plaice we set sail for Dartmouth, where I had been sent as Senior Officer, Landing-Craft, on my return from the Mediterranean. Most of the craft lay in trots up at Dittisham and I had alternated between living aboard one of these more comfortable landing-craft, and spending my nights in a Mark III at Dartmouth. This craft was extremely uncomfortable, but excellent for going ashore, whereas the boats at Dittisham had not been easy to reach, especially as the motor boat I had at my disposal was always breaking down.

Now we had taken a top floor flat in a row of houses overlooking the ferry and the mouth of the river. It had a pleasant view, especially at night, when the lamps on the other side of the river glowed in the water and small craft burned their red and green navigation lights as they passed along and across the river. It was peaceful and self-contained, disturbed only by the sound of hooters down the river, the quiet beat of the ferry engine and the distant noise of an occasional train from the other side.

Our landlord and landlady, Mr and Mrs Ball, were a kindly couple who apparently took a parental interest in our early days of marriage. Biddie was a beginner at cooking, and we fed a good deal on dripping which my mother sent us. She thought it might come in useful, she said.

On one particular evening an attempt was made at a treacle tart. Even from the start it had an unpleasant look about it, and this was not improved when it slipped from the plate my wife was carrying and lay, a soggy mess, on the floor. The alternatives were dripping or a meal out, and the decision was made with little difficulty. Who knows, if the treacle tart had been a success, our venture might have languished there. As it was, we dined out that night as well as one could in 1946, and the story moves on to our meeting with George Allen in the Queen's.

The pub was noisy and crowded, and we had to squeeze our way through to the bar where most of the landing-craft officers were grouped, talking vigorously, awaiting their drinks and demobilisation with equal eagerness. For a wedding present they had given us a handsome silver inkstand in the shape of a capstan, a present which we both treasured.

Over in a corner I recognised Robert Ballantyne, D.S.C., and Larry Osteler, a couple of naval friends, and further away one of the few Army officers in the room, a man called Guy Greville. We jostled our way gradually towards him and he greeted us with a smile. He was a lean, poker-faced person, full of a quiet charm and complete self-assurance. He and his wife Mary had three children and a very large Daimler, and Guy, like myself, had recently been demobilised.

We had both discussed the future, and on several occasions Guy had expounded various ideas on how to make a living; so far his strongest and most consistent belief had been that fishing was the answer. I enquired if he was any further on with his fishing plans.

"A little," he said. "There's certainly money in it. There are plenty of surplus Admiralty craft coming on to the market and I'm going to run over to Bath and get some information on the matter. Why not come along and bring Biddie too? Anyhow, give me a ring if you can."

He left shortly afterwards and we both got up to leave. Just then, as I moved towards the bar with our glasses, a soft voice informed me that it knew just where I could find a boat and where I could catch the fish. I turned, and at my side stood a small, lean man, gazing up at me through steel-rimmed spectacles. His face was tanned by the wind and he wore a seaman's sweater under a black reefer jacket. He drew heavily on his cigarette, smiling all the time; he had shrewd brown eyes like a fox, which watched me closely as he waited for me to speak.

"Oh," I said. "Splendid! Where would that be?"

"Mevagissey, and there's a boat for sale that would just suit you and me." He paused, observing the effect of this last remark. Then he spoke again. He was apparently the mate of an M.F.V. lying on the other side of the river, whose crew was about to be paid off.

"All right," I said. "Meet me here tomorrow night and we'll have a yarn. By the way, I don't know your name."

GEORGE ALLEN

"George Allen, me dear," he replied, and after introductions had been made, we all three went out into the night. George disappeared; we moved away up the steep road and the very steep stairs to our top-floor flat.

"What did you think of George?" I said to Biddie as we lay in bed.

"Bit foxy," she replied, "but rather nice. Are you really going fishing?"

"Oh, I don't know. We'll see what George has got to say about it. Why? Would you like to be a fisherman's wife?"

"Love to," she said, and was asleep.

But I lay awake for a long time afterwards, listening to the river noises and wondering about the future. For the best part of five years I had been at sea and it was something I knew a little about and genuinely loved. It was not really so silly to think of earning a living on the sea. To its possible difficulty I hardly gave a thought. Living in wild and lovely surroundings was far more important. A cottage that commanded all the changing moods of the sea through the year, the to-and-fro traffic of boats, the life of the village, the walks along the cliff-tops—these seemed so fresh and clean beside the grime and aching boredom of a room in Liverpool.

As if in a dream, I could hear the gentle rustle of the curtains as they moved vaguely in the wind. The last ferry had crossed long ago. All was quiet.

The following day the big green Daimler carried us all to Bath. Guy and I discussed boats and it quickly emerged that he was thinking in terms of a large boat, one of the big M.L.s or an M.F.V., and was prepared to pay a much larger sum than I could afford. Neither of us had considered the question of equipment. Guy still stuck to the notion of trawling; I don't think we realised there were other methods of catching fish. The visit to Bath proved fruitless and Guy announced his intention of going to Brixham to see whether he could buy a Brixham trawler.

That evening, when we were both rather tired after our trip, I went down alone to meet George Allen, while Biddie stayed behind to prepare a late bite of food. George had already arrived and in his soft voice asked me what I'd like to drink. We chose a quiet corner of the room and talked about my visit to Bath and George's family, as though shy of what was really uppermost in both our minds—fishing.

"Well," said George at last, when I had asked him to give me some honest and down-to-earth views on the prospects of fishing, "they're making a very good living at Mevagissey, the fish are fetching a good price and I see no reason at all why you and I shouldn't make a good living too. The boat's there waiting. . . ."

"How much?" I asked.

"£700 I think is what Cyril is asking," said George, and he went on to extol the merits of the *Coral*: she was a young boat, well built and easily handled by two men. We would need pilchard nets, a dog and spilter line, and he assured me that I would have no trouble in picking up the ropes. He would show me the way.

"You make it sound easy, George," I murmured.

" 'Ess, me dear," said George as he warmed to his subject. "It's not difficult and in the summer months we can always do a spot of plummeting for mackerel in the early morning."

I listened to all this and couldn't deny that I found it most attractive. The next obvious step was to go down and inspect Mevagissey and I suggested to George that if he was free we should go the following day. He agreed on the spot.

As we got up to leave, he suddenly mentioned as an afterthought that the *Boy Don* was for sale.

"She's the boat they used in the film *Johnny Frenchman*," he added.

I glanced up sharply. "Good Lord, George, we've just seen that film."

"Well," he said, "it was filmed at Mevagissey." For a moment I was back in the warmth of a Lowestoft cinema, watching shots of a wild and rugged coastline, charmed by a fishing village set so naturally into those splendid cliffs. And in that moment I suddenly knew that we would go to Mevagissey and live there. And where could we better begin our married life.

I hurried home, where Biddie had prepared coffee and sandwiches. She watched my face expectantly.

"We'll go," I said. And I told her about my talk with

15

George and our decision to go down to Mevagissey the very next day. She looked slightly crestfallen when I announced that I thought it better that for the first cursory visit George and I should go alone. But I assured her that on this occasion I should make no decision and buy no boat. We would make a full visit together later in the week.

George and I started early the next morning and by eleven o'clock we had reached St Austell. Outside the station we climbed into a bus and after a ten-minute wait set off on the last lap of our journey. I was not impressed with what I could see of St Austell; perhaps I had a picturesque sea town in mind, but my first impression was of a poorly planned town littered with undistinguished buildings. Later I was to grow fond of the place. First impressions are seldom very accurate.

The bus was empty and rattled along for another twenty minutes till we came to Pentewan Sand and the start of a long hill.

"There's the Black Head and Fowey Light," said George as the bus climbed to the top of the hill and motored freely down the other side and into Mevagissey.

We climbed out and walked across the little square past the post office and down to the quay. George, of course, knew everyone and greeted them all. I nodded and smiled and tried to appear casual and normal. These were the people we were proposing to live with and it was vitally important that we should be accepted among them. I would need all the help and advice I could get from them. As we passed little groups of fishermen I was very conscious of their glances. They seemed to be missing very little as they leaned against the walls or stood in little groups. When I came to know them I quickly realised that they miss nothing at all and have a wonderful sense of humour—one of the reasons why I like them so much.

As we passed William Hunkin, the engineer, I saw for the first time the inner and the outer harbour. It was high water and the boats were all at their moorings. We walked

round to Edwards's store, where some more fishermen were sitting on benches along the wall, resembling in their passive acceptance of life the very gulls that stood or strutted in various quarters of the harbour. We stopped and George nodded.

"There she is. That's the *Coral*." Lying a short distance from the quayside was a twenty-seven-foot, half-decked St Ives gig. I could see at a glance, from her good beam, her fullness on the waterline and the fine lift to her bow, that she possessed all the qualities of a staunch sea boat.

I longed to go aboard her there and then, but I could feel the eyes of the fishermen on my back, and they were now no longer talking among themselves. I was relieved when George broke the silence by suggesting we should go home for me to meet his wife.

He lived on the north side of the harbour, along a terrace of cottages. His was at the end, sheltered from most of the winds. We were greeted warmly by Mrs Allen, who at once ordered us to sit down at the table, where plenty of food lay spread out on a clean white tablecloth. It was the first time I had tasted Cornish cream since 1939 and it was as good as ever. As she moved busily around the room attending to our wants, she fired questions at her husband and made brief pithy observations which showed such a shrewd assessment of our venture, that if I had not appreciated her underlying sense of humour, I would have been considerably alarmed. Even so, I was somewhat shaken by her.

"Be you really going to buy that boat?" she asked, and before I had time to reply, she had added with a laugh, "Why, you must be daft. How much is Cyril Hunkin asking?"

"I'm not sure," replied George, "but I've heard tell he's asking £700."

There was an explosive sound from Mrs Allen. "That's a tidy bit of money—what are pilchards fetching?"

"Three-and-three a stone," George replied.

"You are going to have to catch a lot of fish to get that back."

"Cyril's doing well enough in her," said George.

"Yes, but Ken here's not Cyril, and he doesn't know what he's about."

"He'll learn," said George.

"He'll have to," said his wife, glancing sharply at me, though I detected some anxiety in her eyes.

18

I sat quietly listening, feeling really rather stupid; I knew that much of what she said was very true.

Mrs Allen was a realist; her aggressive attitude towards this venture only sprang from her deep suspicion of the sea and her knowledge of the difficulties of wresting a living from it. Since she was born and bred in Mevagissey, she could not understand how someone from up-country could come along and imagine he could own a boat and earn a living. To add fuel to the fire, her husband intended joining the venture. Despite all that, however, she was most welcoming and kind, and when we left to return to Dartmouth she wished me luck.

"Have you anywhere to live?" she asked.

"No," I replied, and she at once kindly offered to go and see Mrs Church of Beach Road.

Three days later Biddie, George and I set out for Mevagissey. Once again I walked past William, the engineer, and through to the inner harbour. Again I could feel the keen glances of the fishermen and could well imagine the small groups discussing our venture with some amusement. I had little doubt that what I had in mind was known throughout the village.

"Do 'e like it, Biddie, me old dear?" said George.

One glance at her face told me that the village had come up to her expectations. She wanted to be shown the *Coral*, but I could only bring myself to point her out briefly. We would not stop and examine her carefully, I said, as it would all look so obvious what we were about. Somehow I did not want this.

We wandered to the outer harbour, where the luggers were already lying ready for the night's fishing. From there we climbed the steep steps to the top of Polkirt Hill and, leaning on the wall, we looked down on the two harbours. Again I pointed out the *Coral* and we were able to inspect her in greater privacy. The more I saw of her, the more I liked the look of her.

It was a fine, windy day, with great splashes of blue sky

under which the long white clouds raced away, reflecting their passage on the sea. Across the harbour, a dinghy with five-gallon drums of fuel aboard was being slowly sculled out to a lugger. The man stood in the stern, gently stroking his oar backwards and forwards quite effortlessly. I made a mental note that I must learn how to scull, for even I could see that rowing would be out of place in such a community. On a wall of the inner harbour a crew were stretching their nets to dry, having barked and tarred them. Below us a long-liner was unloading her catch and the chatter of the crew and the idle beat of her diesel could be clearly heard.

On the other side, the fishermen's cottages rose steeply up to the coastguard station and appeared to be topped by a green field. The Black Head thrust out its round hump to sea and further to the north lay Fowey headland caught in sunlight. Even as we watched, the sunlight seemed to move along that splendid coastline, touching one headland after another. The wind blew even stronger and the bay filled with white horses.

But in spite of the strength of the wind, George assured me that the boats would be going out tonight; for the wind was offshore, and in the lee of the land there would be no sea to speak of. It was the easterly wind that was really bad for Mevagissey fishing, a fact I was to learn by experience in the near future.

We walked down Polkirt Hill, along the one and only street, till we came to the square and the post office, where we had left our cases. The genial Mr Clarke beamed and greeted us warmly.

"Come and see us when you've got settled in," he called over the counter.

We carried our suitcases up Cliff Walk, past the coast-guard station, till we came to the green field that I had seen from the other side of the harbour. We stopped to get our breath and peered over the wall and down the great cliffs. I would have stayed longer, but George was anxious to hand us over to Mrs Church. In any case, I had important business with Cyril Hunkin and the sooner that was settled the better.

We followed the line of the cliff till we came to a row of houses facing due south. The end house stood right on the edge of the cliff. Ours was four along. We passed through a low swing-gate and before we had time to knock, the door was opened by a very small white-haired lady, whose glasses rested on the end of her nose. Behind her stood her husband, bent and smiling.

"Come in, my dears," she said. "Are you going to have a cup of tea as well, George?"

"No, thanks, me old sweetheart," he replied, "but I'll be up at six o'clock to fetch Ken."

Mrs Church began by showing us our room downstairs and then the bedroom.

"The last person who slept here," she said, indicating the double bed with the feather mattress, "was Françoise Rosay. Did you ever see a film called *Johnny Frenchman*?"

"Why, yes," we both exclaimed, and once again I caught a glimpse of the pattern into which everything seemed to fit; and it resembled the sea, this pattern. Both were always on the move, always shifting, fine weather changing to bad, ups and downs, variable, inexplicable; one moment all sails set and running free, the next riding out the storm and meeting troubles. Acceptance of hardships and pleasures, acceptance of bad weather as well as good; the fishermen had known all this for generations, and I was already learning it.

"Well, I'll leave you to unpack," said Mrs Church, "and there'll be some tea when you come down."

We thanked her and walked over to our bedroom window. We looked over the green field and the top of the coastguard station and away across the bay to Chapel Point, upon which stood three isolated white houses. It was a fine picture and on a day of such shifting light and shade we could feel nothing but great happiness.

George arrived after tea and we went down to 2 Chapel Street, where Cyril Hunkin lived. His wife opened the door and we all went into a kitchen warmed by an open range. Cyril was friendly and with a smile asked me how I liked Mevagissey.

"Very much," I replied.

" 'Ess," he said. "It's a handsome place, especially in the summer. Are you going to live here?"

"I want to," I said, "and buy a boat." And I asked him there and then whether he was thinking of selling the *Coral* and if so, what price he was asking.

"Seven hundred pounds," said Cyril, smiling all the time, "but I'm not particularly anxious to sell the boat, as we've been doing very well of late with the dogs."

A business-man, I suppose, would have offered him a lower price and settled for a figure between the two. But I have never been able to haggle; this requires a certain toughness of character I do not possess. I have always taken people at their face value, and if I want to buy something and the price is high, I either accept the price or decline the article.

I wanted the *Coral*, so I bought her. Although I afterwards learnt I had paid a high price, I never regretted a penny of the money. Indeed, when the sad time came for me to part with her, I dropped only £20. £20 for nineteen months sailing in the *Coral* was not expensive.

As I wrote out a cheque for £700, I did think it wise to enquire about the state of her engines.

"They're in good condition," Cyril assured me. "She had a reconditioned Thornycroft Handy Billy put in this month, and there is nothing wrong with the Kelvin. The boat is thoroughly sound and I'll give you any help I can," he added.

He was still smiling when we left, a smile that concealed shrewdness and a sharp mind.

I sighed. That was that. I at once suggested to George that we should go and have a proper look at the *Coral* now, as it was low water and we could walk out to her moorings.

I felt glad it was dark, because I did not want everyone to

see me go aboard the boat for the first time. Despite the fact I had been afloat for the best part of five years during the war and had commanded my own tank landing-craft, I still felt very much a novice in the eyes of the fishermen. There was only time for a cursory glance at the boat; the tide was on the make and had already reached the *Coral*. Indeed, we had to leave in a hurry to avoid wet feet, but at least I had been aboard her, and tomorrow I could take a good look around.

I said good night to George and climbed homewards with half a moon to light my path. At the top I looked out over the cliff and saw the lights of the fishing boats out in the bay. The wind was not so strong as I turned into it and walked up Beach Road.

CHAPTER TWO

Removal by Sea

My first thought on waking concerned my dress. I had some leather sea-boots and a thick white polo sweater. With some old flannels tucked into the leather sea-boots I suppose I did not look too bad. Biddie observed that I looked just the part. I wondered about this.

With a wave and as jaunty a step as I could manage, I set off across the field and down to the harbour. All went well until I reached the path, where my new leather soles began to slip on the steep gradient. To make matters worse, the sea-boots were stiff—the leather was brand new and they had never been worn—and each time I took a step forward, it sounded like a guardsman on parade.

My God, I thought, they will all know I'm on the way; and sure enough as I reached the first wall overlooking the harbour, there they were all assembled leaning against the wall. With one accord their heads turned to discover what on earth was coming their way.

"Good morning," I said as I passed.

"Mornin', Cap'n, mornin'," they replied. How dearly I would have liked to lean against that wall and talk with them! But as yet I had not earned that privilege. I knew I should have to go through a period of inspection when they watched to see what I wanted and what I intended to do.

I moved down to the quayside, desperately hoping George would be about; for having arrived at the harbour, I really wasn't at all certain what to do next. I passed Pawlyn's store and to my relief saw George, complete with his black beret, waiting under Edwards's store.

"No more lyin' abed now, me old dear," said George, looking at his watch significantly.

I felt slightly irritated at this remark, for I was anxious to make a good impression from the start.

Cyril had been fishing for J. B. Edwards when he owned the *Coral*, and it was assumed that I should continue to fish for him.

"Come and meet J.B.," said George, and I followed him up a dark wooden stairway, smelling of tar, and turned left through a door into an office.

J.B. was old, white-haired and affable.

"So you'm agoing fishin'?" he asked with friendly amusement creasing his face. His daughter Jean, standing behind him, gave me confidence.

"Yes, I hope to," I replied.

"It's hard work, you know; long hours and often not much money in it. Have you got any gear?"

"No," I replied and George added that we were going to buy a fleet of pilchard nets that afternoon.

"He'd better have Cyril's old loft; it'll be handy with her moorings just underneath. Has he got any fishing clothes? He'll want a smock, sea-boots and an oilskin, I'll fix him up with those. He'll also need a permit for a thermos."

The latter was apparently so scarce that it could only be obtained by this means.

"Don't forget to tell your wife," said J.B.'s daughter, "that you are entitled to extra rations of meat and cheese."

Once out of his office we turned left and, mounting another few steps, we entered Cyril's loft. A fisherman's loft is a fascinating place: a confusion of lines, ropes, nets, old sails, spars, dan buoys, tubs of line, and the clean, ever-present smell of tar. Cyril's loft was not particularly well served by window space, but I soon found that most of the lofts were poorly lit and that mine, if anything, was better than the others in this respect. There was another loft above mine, owned by Edgar Husband, and I could hear the men and their quick snatches of conversation as they moved about.

Outside again the wind was freshening from the east, and I gathered from the odd remarks I could hear and understand, that it was unlikely that the boats would be going out tonight, as it was "giving bad weather," an expression I was to hear many times.

"Let's go aboard," said George. "We'll use Cyril's dinghy." Again I could feel the eyes of the fishermen watching us intently. A small fishing harbour is a wonderful place for just sitting and watching; and here was I providing something dramatic to watch, a "proper Joe" coming to attempt a job of work they had been doing for generations.

"Unship the legs," said George, "and I'll start up the Handy Billy." He handed me a spanner and I soon had the legs inboard.

I wasn't clear how she was moored. There was a narrow three-foot piece of wood lying on the deckboards of the net-room, from each end of which led a rope which after a short length joined a chain. This chain passed through the fair-leads fore and aft and was secured inboard.

George had started the starboard engine and now came forward. He tossed overboard the narrow piece of wood and told me to let go the forward piece of chain and he'd let go aft. With a splash the boat was free. George took the wheel and put her astern. With a kick ahead and the wheel over we were under way for the first time. We threaded our path through the toshers, twenty-foot one-man boats, and past the luggers in the outer harbour, till we came to the harbour entrance with Mevagissey Light on our starboard hand.

"You take her," said George, "and I'll start the Kelvin."

So for the first time I took the wheel of the *Coral* and looked ahead over her blunt, uplifted bows to the Black Head and Fowey. I felt the keen easterly wind on my cheeks and knew in that moment that the decision I had taken was right.

I could hear George muttering from below, then suddenly the outer engine raced to life for a few moments, spluttered and died away. George appeared with an ordinary oil can and filled it with petrol from a tap off the main petrol tank for the Thornycroft.

"I'll prime her again and she'll be away," he muttered to himself. A minute later the Kelvin again burst into life and I could feel the boat thrust ahead and lift her bows even higher. With both engines going full ahead we motored splendidly. The wind was now blowing strongly from the east, and as we cleared Chapel Point and opened up the Dodman I could see that there would be plenty of sea a mile or so out. We both ducked as she snubbed into a sea, and spray flew back over the boat as we turned and headed for the Black Head.

I handed over the wheel to George and went to inspect the engines. I have never been mechanically minded and these two noisy machines looked most frightening. As I knelt in the confined engine-room, the smell from the paraffin, petrol and bilges hit me full in the face. I could not help speculating on the extreme difficulties involved in effecting a repair at sea. There were only two loose boards over the two propeller shafts on which one would have to kneel or squat to work, and I could see clearly that there would be every chance of burning one's fingers on the hot exhaust and other parts of the engines. I came up, slightly chastened, for some fresh air.

We were closing the shore rapidly and could see the sea piling up on the Black Head. We turned and headed for Mevagissey Light. On the top of the cliffs I glimpsed our house, and suddenly feeling ravenously hungry I wondered what we were having for lunch. When we were approaching the harbour entrance George switched over the Kelvin to petrol and then, as we entered the outer harbour, he stopped her. With the main engine silent and the Thornycroft throttled down, it seemed very quiet as we chugged into the inner harbour to pick up the *Coral's* moorings.

That afternoon I purchased my fleet of pilchard nets from Gordon Barron. I bought six nets at twelve pounds a net and paid two pounds for the corks and buffs. It was then that I first met Peter Barron; I was deeply impressed by a face which revealed a lifetime of resignation and patience. He was white-haired and gentle of manner and when I watched him still clearing and baiting up his never-ending spilter line, at the end of a day that had begun at two in the morning, I could see he was ready to go ashore and lead an easier life.

In the evening Biddie and I strolled to the cliff edge and looked out at the boats which were lying to their nets, their mast-head lights flickering in the darkness. It suddenly occurred to us that we might bring down all our belongings from Dartmouth by sea in the *Coral*. It would save money, give me an opportunity to know the *Coral*, and provided there were no March gales offer a pleasant passage up the coast. George was amenable and it was decided we should sail early on 27 February.

We fuelled the *Coral* and took aboard an extra twenty gallons of petrol and paraffin in five-gallon drums. Biddie made sandwiches for us all and although we took thermos-flasks of tea, we also carried fresh water, milk, sugar and tea for the primus stove we had aboard.

By seven o'clock we had cleared the harbour and were on our way. The wind was still in the east and blustery at that; we set course for the Rame, bumping and slithering across the easterly seas. Momentarily, before she slipped into the trough, the *Coral's* exhausts would gurgle with delight. The sun shone; the sea sparkled and occasionally slapped the bow of the *Coral* with a friendly blow, sending spray flying across the boat. The salt was on our lips and there was good clean air to breathe. What more could we want?

"How do 'ee like it, me old sweetheart?" shouted George above the engines to my wife. She was up in the bows and her answer lay in her smile.

We decided to give the boat a good clean-up while Biddie took the wheel. I gave her a course to steer and she soon understood that it was inadvisable to chase the lubber's point.

Meanwhile, we took up the bottom boards and cleaned the channels through the boat's timbers which were blocked by pilchard scales. We scooped up quantities of fish scales, oil and slime and got her a good deal cleaner. As I stood in the net-room I glanced up at Biddie, who was sitting on the engine-coaming steering a good course and obviously enjoying herself.

"Very smelly," she shouted above the engines.

I nodded and glanced down at the *Coral's* timbers. She was very strongly built and had for a time been pilot boat of the Scilly Isles. She was ideally constructed for crabbing, but for netting and lining she needed more draught. I was to hear the fishermen remark on several occasions that the *Coral* was a fine boat, but she'd flap like a skate in any weather and wouldn't easily ride to the lines or the nets. Most of the Mevagissey boats were much deeper draughted, with the result that they held more steady in the water and responded better to their mizzens. The *Coral* had been built on the north coast, where there was a great run when the tide came in and the danger to deep-draughted boats was that they might snap their legs and go over on their sides. This would never happen to a shallow-draughted boat. I was also to discover how much harder it is to scrape and paint the bottom of a shallow-draughted boat. One must find a suitable beach and list her over so as to get right under her.

We had now been running for about three hours and were off Looe Island when we hungrily decided to have our sandwiches. George had an enormous Cornish pasty and told Biddie that Charlie Hicks baked them in his 120-year-old oven. The fishermen's wives took their lunches to him to be cooked. It always intrigued me to watch the wives carrying their beautifully prepared lunches to this fine old oven.

We had sixty miles to cover, and I estimated we would not be off Dartmouth for about ten hours. The wind was still strong, but the weather was fine and looked as though it was settling. By eleven o'clock we were off the Rame and had altered course for Bolt Head. As we crossed Plymouth Sound a destroyer was coming up on our starboard quarter. George was at the wheel and Biddie was up forward. I could see the ship was approaching at a good fifteen knots, rapidly overhauling us. I glanced at George and mentioned the fact that the destroyer was closing us fast and if we held this course we would either just cross her bows or she would cross ours.

"I should haul off, George," I said.

"It's our right of way," he replied, and said something about two points abaft the beam. I looked again and saw now that she was very close indeed. I could not believe he would still hold his course.

"Look out, George," I shouted, but it was too late and for one awful moment I thought the destroyer was going to cut us down.

As it was she swept past our stern so close that I could almost have touched her stem with a broom-handle. I could hear a voice from the bridge shouting at us, glimpse some sailors in the waist of the ship pause in their duties and stare and then she was past and we were being rocked by her wash.

I was very angry, for it had been an unwarranted risk and a very close thing. I should have insisted on giving the destroyer the right of way, but I was going to work with George and I had to show my trust in his judgment. Nevertheless it had been shaken.

At 2.30 we had opened up Start Point. I knew there was broken water off this point, and had a look through my binoculars at the headland, which was now about two miles away. There was little doubt that there was a good deal of lumpy water, and as we drew nearer I told George it would be advisable to give the point a wide berth. But he insisted we would be quite safe if we were 300 yards offshore.

"I don't like it, George," I said, still hoping he would alter course to the east.

"It's all right, me dear. There's no point in adding another three or four miles by going outside, and you're not scared of a bit of sea." I made no reply and we motored on in silence.

Biddie was again up forward and only her shoulders were outside the boat.

"Hang on," I shouted as we neared the race. Then we

31

were in it and a most uncomfortable ten minutes followed while lumps and chunks of water hit the boat from all angles. But she was a stout little boat and, apart from giving us all an eyeful of spray, she bounced her way through. I could see the coastguard watching through binoculars from the headland, but we were on the last lap now and the sea was flattening all the time.

I should, of course, have insisted on going well outside, but something held me back. This was not the Navy, where the Captain is answerable to his Lords and Commissioners, the Admiralty, but a fishing boat with a skipper answerable to no one but the owner, in this case me. I had to learn from George and work with him and, therefore, I realised that he should not feel I was questioning his every move.

By five o'clock we were entering the mouth of the Dart and there was our flat and here was the ferry coming across. We cut off the Kelvin and motored gently up the river, past the Royal Naval College, till we rounded a bend and sighted the trots of landing-craft, of which only a short time ago I had been Senior Officer.

We made fast the *Coral* and climbed aboard to be warmly greeted by the officers. After a good wash and a meal it was fun sitting in the warmth of the wardroom. But this was the life I had just left and already I felt that I was closer to the sea than I had ever been as a rating or an officer.

The next morning we took the *Coral* down the river to call on Mr and Mrs Ball and collect our belongings. Mrs Ball insisted on our staying to tea. Her husband had spent all his life at sea in cable-laying vessels and I brought him a pound of leaf tobacco, which he apparently enjoyed more than anything else.

Night had fallen when we began to carry our goods and chattels down to the *Coral*, where we stowed everything in the net room, lit by the fishing lights. We had secured the *Coral* near the Customs Office and there were a great number of other small craft moored around us.

I started up the Thornycroft myself, a feat I was rather

proud of; I had received a full hour's instruction that morning by one of the motor mechanics from the landing-craft.

"Knock her in," shouted George after our line had gone, and no sooner had we begun to move than we fouled our propeller with a rope. Seizing a gaff, I was just able to reach some vertical wooden steps and pull her stern into the side.

The next half-hour was by no means enjoyable. With George and Biddie holding the *Coral* clear of my head which was between the boat and the jetty, I went down the wooden ladder up to my thighs in the water and did my best to free the propeller. But the rope was bar taut. There was no chance of my succeeding and quite a fair chance of my head being crushed.

Tired and rather depressed, I emerged from the cold water and climbed aboard the boat.

"We'll start the Kelvin," I said and, priming her generously, she fired first go.

."Knock her in," shouted George again and as I bent forward over the Kelvin to tighten one of the priming valves, I was suddenly thrown violently forward, hitting my head against the engine-room deck-head and smashing the light.

"What the hell's that?" I shouted as I knocked her out of gear.

"Can't see," said George, and small wonder, for he still had his fishing lights on and consequently could see nothing ahead. I switched them off and peered fiercely into the darkness. All I could pick out were vague shapes of boats. Everything seemed in order and I hoped that we had only hit the boat, if it was a boat, a glancing blow. I put the engine ahead again and very carefully we motored clear of any more obstacles and up the Dart to the landing-craft. We would plainly not be able to sail the next day for Mevagissey; the *Coral* would have to be beached so that we could free her propeller.

The following morning I was lying half-awake when I

was suddenly jerked to full consciousness by the ominous words, "Is Lieutenant Shearwood aboard?"

A rating came down and told me there were two men on deck who wanted to see me. I dressed quickly and went up top.

"Good morning, sir. Is that your boat alongside?"

"It is," I answered.

"I believe you moored her outside the Customs Office last night and left shortly before seven."

"Yes; that is right," I said and waited for what I knew would come next.

"Did you hit anything?"

"We hit something," I replied.

"You certainly did," they said in unison. "The one and only pilot boat. If we hadn't heard the crash and come out at once she'd have sunk. As it was we were just able to shift her pegs over and list her damaged planks clear of the water. We've brought her up for you to have a look at her."

There was no doubt that we had hit her fair and square, but I was surprised we had done so much damage.

"Well, come and have a cup of coffee," I suggested. They had known me when I was Senior Officer, Landing-Craft, and, considering the circumstances, they were extremely genial. It was finally decided that they should obtain an estimate from the boat-builders. It cost me £48 and I paid up on the spot, never questioning the estimate or considering insurance. Although the boat was insured, it was not in my name.

That afternoon we beached the *Coral* on the Dart's wooded banks and freed the propeller. She lay in thick mud, which made walking difficult and the task of freeing the half-buried propeller far from easy. But we got her free and floated her off by tea-time. In the evening we took some officers in the *Coral* up the river to a little inn by the river's edge, where we had sandwiches and beer and talked till closing time.

By six o'clock the next morning we had slipped and were

34

on our way down the river. It was a cold and beautifully
clear morning and the *Coral's* decks glistened with dew in
the early morning light. Ahead of us lay the mouth of the
river and the open sea, a very pale grey and flat calm.
There was hardly any movement as we set course for Start
Point, a course which I was determined would take us well
outside the point this time.

Our passage home could not have been more fun. The
sun shone, there was not a cloud in the sky and the sea was

calm the whole way down. We lit the primus and boiled a
kettle and made a pot of tea. We lay full length on the
Coral's warm deck and drank our tea and watched the
distant coast line. Suddenly we were startled by a shout
from George. "Gannets," he cried and pointed over the
starboard bow. "There they go." We saw them for the first
time plummeting vertically into the sea, sending up a small
splash like a tiny bomb explosion. Soon we came to
distinguish these birds from seagulls, whose flight and
shape are crude in comparison. Gannets are torpedo-shaped
and their wings are tipped with black, but apart from these
distinguishing features they always appeared to me to look
whiter against the background of the sea. To a fisherman it
is a thrilling sight to see gannets diving ; it is a sure sign that
fish are in the vicinity.

The gannet will feed till it is too heavy to leave the water, and if a boat approaches, the bird will, in its fear, vomit up the fish it has been eating and the crew can then discover whether the food has been sprats or pilchards.

Many times while serving in H.M.S. *Montrose* I was called a gannet, though perhaps not quite so simply or politely. In fact, I was not allowed my mess savings because I ate so much. But it was well worth forgoing the savings if one could snatch a great hunk of bread and jam before going on watch.

We had come down with the ebb tide and were entering the harbour by three o'clock that afternoon, having made an excellent run. There was just sufficient water in the inner harbour for us to moor the *Coral*. We would have to wait till the evening, when the inner harbour would be full, before we could bring the *Coral* alongside and offload our belongings straight into a taxi.

We said goodbye to George and made our way home. We walked up Cliff Walk and found the fishermen were still leaning over the same old wall, watching and talking. As we came up to them one of them turned and spoke to us.

"Have a good trip?" he asked.

"Yes, a splendid one," we replied. He was small and seventy years old, with the bluest eyes I have ever seen. He was well turned out and wore his cap straight on his head; his coarse blue serge trousers were neatly pressed and his thick-soled boots were highly polished. His name was Willie Rollins and I was to see much of him in the future.

"Missus enjoy it?" he asked.

"Yes, it was lovely," replied Biddie.

They were now all watching us with a friendly interest.

"We saw lots of gannets coming down," I ventured.

"Whereabouts did you see 'em, me old dear?" asked Albert of the *Pride of the West*.

"Most of them were between Looe Island and Fowey."

"You'd better get them nets aboard," said Bill Rollins, Willie's son, and they all laughed.

"We're going to put them aboard tomorrow, all being well."

"Proper job," they all said. "Proper job." And we continued our way up to Beach Road, tired and full of good sea air, feeling that, despite one or two tricky episodes, the *Coral* really did belong to us now.

CHAPTER THREE

A Night of Pilchard Driving

On the first day of March we hauled our nets aboard the *Coral*. J. B. Edwards lent me his lorry to transfer them from Gordon Barron's loft to the boat. Gordon and George loaded the six nets on to the lorry with George holding the headrope and Gordon on the leech, which is the name for the bottom part of the net. There seemed to me to be an incredible amount of net, and in actual fact it runs to 720 yards; despite the lightness of the fine Egyptian cotton thread, it was obvious that the six nets were a considerable weight.

Along the top of a pilchard net, 120 yards long, lies the headrope to which the nets are attached. Into this headrope corks are fixed at short intervals, and at longer intervals are strops which are three-fathom lengths of rope with a corbal at the end. A corbal is simply a bunch of corks tied together which helps to hold up the nets in the water. I had seven buffs, white, inflated, balloon-like objects about twice the size of a football, which also served to hold up the nets and give an indication of their lie.

The meshes in a pilchard net are a little under an inch square and the nets lead out from the boat in one straight line and hang down in the water to a depth of 40 to 50 feet. The fish swim into the net and are caught by their gills in the meshes. Two men can shoot the nets with little difficulty in a boat like the *Coral*, and I remember on one occasion a fisherman in a tosher going out and shooting his nets single-handed. It was a Sunday and his partner, on principle, would not go to sea. But a bigger boat takes a larger crew and more than twenty nets.

Ideally, in shooting nets from a lugger, one man stands at the wheel to tend the engines, one goes on the headrope and one on the leech. The other members of the crew are always ready for any emergency. It sometimes happens that a corbal strop will not come out cleanly from the net-room, in which case the headrope must be held until the corbal strop is cleared. In fine weather the man at the headrope is usually able to hold on, but in any wind and sea the rope might easily be torn from his hands. In such a case the man at the wheel, having first knocked out the engine, will grab hold of the headrope as well, while one of the other hands clears the fouled corbal strop ; then the shooting of the nets can continue.

Accidents at sea happen very suddenly and quickly and if a line or a net should take charge, a man might be lost overboard and swept away into the darkness without warning. Weighed down by oilskins and sea-boots, he would have little chance.

But we were a two-man boat, and as I stood watching George and Gordon haul aboard the last net I realised how little I knew. It was, in fact, the first time in my life I had ever set eyes on a fishing net ; I knew nothing of how they worked and I had never seen a pilchard. All this I would have to learn gradually by experience. This would begin in a few hours, for that night we were going out pilchard driving for the first time and perhaps we would earn some money.

The term pilchard driving originates from the feud between the seine-netters and the drift-netters. Long before drift nets had come into use, pilchards had been caught in great quantities by seine nets. In one year alone it is recorded that 3,500 tons of pilchards were exported from Mevagissey. But from the beginning of the nineteenth century the number of drift boats began to increase till in 1839 there were 360 men seine fishing and 60 using drift nets, and great was the enmity between the two camps. In the same year several of the drifters were brought before the justices

39

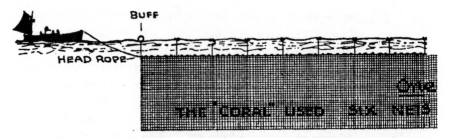

for shooting their nets too near the shore, contrary to an Act
of Parliament in 1662, which laid down that no fishing was
to be within a league and a half of any cove in Cornwall from
the first of June till the last of November.

But there was no stopping the increasing number of
drifters in spite of the seine-netters' strong opposition and
repeated accusations that the drifters were breaking up the
shoals and driving the pilchards away. "Pilchard drivers"
was their bitter cry, and the name has stuck.

At twelve o'clock we brought the *Coral* alongside opposite the lorry and began to haul the nets down from the
vehicle into the net-room. I was on the headrope, George
on the leech.

"Not so fast, Ken," said George softly. "There's a good
deal more leech than headrope; and don't put the headrope
all in a bunch, but spread it out alongside the engine room
bulkhead."

We hauled it aboard and the lorry drove off. I took hold
of two empty five-gallon drums of petrol and paraffin and
climbed on to the quay to walk to William and get them
filled.

"Take Cyril's dinghy," George called after me. Cyril
had very kindly allowed us to use his dinghy until I had
obtained one. I jumped aboard the *Coral* again.

"I don't think I will, George. I can't scull," I said rather
awkwardly. George looked up and smiled understandingly.

"You'll have to learn," he said. "But don't worry; we'll
both go. I'll scull and you can watch."

We put the five-gallon drums aboard the dinghy and

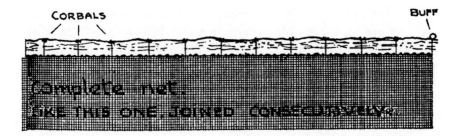

George sculled her across to William, while I sat in the bow
and watched the seemingly easy figure-of-eight movement.

William had a big, round, heavy face and body and was
invariably dressed in dungarees stained dark with oil and
constant work. He always wore a cap, and the only time I
saw him without a cigarette in his mouth was when he was
in the process of removing one and lighting another. For
all his size, he was remarkably agile, and at his long bench,
littered with tools, engine parts and a multitude of other
objects, he would work with great speed, briskly seizing
the implement he required and answering the constant
questions of the fishermen, who came in and out all day,
with a speed and accuracy which indicated an excellent brain.

He broke off from his work at his bench, wiped his hands
on a rag, rolled his cigarette across his mouth and began to
fill our drums.

"Going out tonight?" he asked with a twinkle in his eye,
and before I had time to reply he was busy answering a
question from one of the Lakemans who was standing in
the doorway. I often wondered whether William made any
money, for although he worked very fast and long hours,
he charged very little for his labours.

We fuelled the *Coral*, put her to her moorings and went
home to lunch. I had acquired from J.B. an ordinary fishing
smock, long fisherman's thigh-boots and a stiff yellow oilskin, all in one piece, which reached to my ankles. I had
bought in addition two pairs of blue dungarees. After an
early cup of tea I waved Biddie goodbye and with a tin of
food under my arm and a thermos in my right hand, I set

off for my first night's fishing. I felt much less conspicuous in my sea-boots, blue dungarees and brown smock, in spite of their newness.

When I reached the quay, fishermen were still emerging from the narrow alleys between the cottages which all lead down to the harbour. The various crews were gathering in little groups and some had already gone aboard and started up their engines.

George had pulled Cyril's dinghy alongside and we were about to go down into the boat when a thick, barrel-chested fisherman came over and spoke to me. I found him difficult to follow, for he talked at great speed and very earnestly.

"Now look 'ee here, me old Cap'n, you've got a shallow-drafted boat there, so pump her out as you pull the nets aboard, otherwise you'll get water into your fly-pans which will wet your magnetos and stop your engines." I had barely time to nod, let alone speak, before he went on: "The wireless is giving bad weather and the wind's gone round to the east, so my advice to you, old Cap'n, is to stick with the fleet, for it's going to come in dirty tonight."

I was starting to thank him when again he rushed on: "You don't mind me telling you, but you're new to this and we want to help you."

He was already halfway down the steps when he turned once more, "Don't forget, me old hearty, pump her out and stick with the fleet."

I was touched by Charlie Pearce's advice; it was, I felt, not only sound but he had been sincerely anxious to help. I glanced across at George and saw that he had not really approved of Charlie's remarks.

"Let's get aboard," he said, and we climbed down the steps and into the dinghy, which George sculled the short distance to the *Coral*. We unshipped the legs, started first the Thornycroft Handy Billy and, when we had cleared the inner harbour, the Kelvin. It was five o'clock, with not much daylight left as we passed Mevagissey Light. The boats ahead of us were heading north for the Gribbin.

42

I took our tins of food and put them up forward in the cuddy, the tiny forecastle which contained our twelve-volt battery and two shelves. One man could take shelter in here, but hardly two. I closed the sliding door and looked up. There was nothing ahead but open sea. The rest of the boats were off our port bow, heading away from us on a north-easterly course. I clambered aft and, standing in the engine-room space, leant forward and asked George why we were not following the fleet.

"I know where they are tonight, Ken," he said with quiet conviction, and continued on the same course, leaning forward over the wheel, peering eagerly ahead over the *Coral's* bows, looking for gannets.

"Yes, George, but Charlie's last words were to stick with the fleet."

"Never mind what Charlie said. We'll run down and have a look outside the Dodman."

"The forecast's bad."

"We'll not go far," said George.

I said nothing, but I was far from happy. Once again I was faced with the difficult decision of whether to take charge myself or give George his head. Apart from the fact that I had never seen a pilchard net shot or hauled, and consequently would have to rely entirely on George, there was the additional difficulty that we would be coming in by night and I was unacquainted with the coast.

I looked astern and saw we were now quite on our own, already some four or five miles to the south of the other boats. We were abreast of the Gwineas and in the fast-fading light it looked a great granite beast of a rock, as menacing as the humped back of a lion crouching for its prey. Ahead of us the scarred face of the Dodman stretched up to a sky grey and no less threatening.

We motored down to Hemmick Bay, but in the grey light could see no gannets, so we brought the *Coral* round and headed east until we were some three miles south-east of the Dodman.

43

"We'll shoot here," said George. "Shut off the Kelvin," and with the main engine silent and the Thornycroft just turning over, we very slowly nosed our way round till we were before the wind and the sea.

The first white buff hit the water with a smack and we began to shoot the net, George on the headrope, myself on the leech. In order to keep the net square, I had to shoot the net faster than George. At times George gave the *Coral* a kick ahead to keep enough way on the boat and to ensure the nets were lying in a straight line. He would pause occasionally and hold on to the headrope while the weight of the boat pulled the nets out.

Shooting the leech was not difficult, but, like all movements in fishing, it required a rhythm; so did pulling or shooting nets, baiting or clearing lines. Like the mountaineer, one had to obtain this rhythm in order to combat the long hours of tedious but skilled work. To rush at the job would be fatal.

I was to learn too that if I was to escape the tedium of repetitive work, I must develop some mental avenue of escape. I was fortunate in having George Allen with me in this respect, for he was always willing to talk and there was much that I could learn from him.

I was sweating as the last net went overboard. George hoisted our masthead lamp while I took the boatrope forward, which is the line attached to the headrope of the last net, and passed it through the fairleads and secured it inboard. The *Coral's* bow swung round into the wind and sea and we lay to our nets with the engines quiet and the peace only broken by the sound of the wind and the sea. The daylight was very nearly gone and the stars were hidden by low clouds. To the east it looked very black and the wind was increasing.

"We'll eat," said George and we took out our tins and, leaning against the boat's side, looked out into the darkness and drank our tea. Occasionally we talked, but for the most part we watched the shadowy gulls as they floated up and over the seas, listened to their quiet squawk as they fluttered above the nets to take up a new position. George drew heavily on his cigarette and the glow revealed his eager, aquiline features. I began to whistle softly.

"Damme, what be 'ee about?" he said. "Do 'ee want to whistle up more wind?"

The boat gave a sudden lurch as a sea lifted her more quickly and passed on its way shorewards. It was as if the *Coral* were tugging impatiently, at the nets. I felt it was time we began to haul them, for it was beginning to rain and visibility was closing down. George must have had the same thought, for he started to put on his oilskin. I had difficulty in getting into mine; it was new and very stiff. Once inside, no matter how much water came over the boat, I knew I should remain dry, for I was encased from neck to ankles.

We shipped the roller, over which we would pull the nets inboard, on the starboard side, the side from which all fishing boats operate their gear.

"I'll hoist the mizzen," George called out, "you start the Handy Billy." She started first time and I turned to give George a hand. The sail was halfway up.

"The bloody thing's jammed," he shouted. "Here, catch hold of this rope and pull hard." There was a sudden sharp twang as the rope parted and half the sail dropped over the stern into the sea. We both swore as we groped in the dark for the wet sail, leaning over the stern, which was one moment lifted clear of the sea and the next dropping back into the following wave. When we had the sail aboard we did not attempt to hoist it again, for the wind was freshening all the time and there were squalls of rain.

"Now look," said George. "You're going to pull the headrope and I'll pull the leech. We'll try and run these nets in without using the engine, but if you do have to use it, for goodness sake watch out you don't foul a corbal strop. The sooner we get these nets inboard the better."

He went forward, cast off the rope holding us to the nets

45

and, lying back on the rope, pulled the *Coral* along till we came to the headrope, which he passed to me. I could see very little of the lie of the nets as I peered into the darkness and began the back-aching task of pulling the headrope.

"Watch out for that corbal strop," shouted George. "Here they come. See 'em, Ken?" and looking down into the water lit up by our fishing lights, I saw the silvery pilchards caught in the black meshes, watched the fish hanging from the net as it came clear of the water, saw them pulled over the roller, some dropping back into the sea to float clear, only to be swooped on by the screaming gulls and torn to pieces. The noise of the birds was harsh to the ears and never ceased while the nets were being hauled. One had to shout in order to make oneself heard and they were so close to the boat that the beat of their wings fanned our cheeks. They were not in the least afraid and would insolently perch on the *Coral* at arm's length to watch the proceedings.

I found the headrope fearfully hard to pull, for the boat would not keep up to the line now that our mizzen was out of action. I was, in fact, pulling the boat broadside on to the nets.

"It's no good, George. I can't make any headway on this rope. I'll have to use the engine."

Hanging on the headrope with my right hand, I knocked in the gear and put the wheel a few spokes over to starboard. I felt the weight of the headrope lessen and began to take in the slack.

"Knock her out," shouted George. "Midships, look out for that corbal."

I knocked the gear back with my left hand into what I imagined was neutral, in actual fact I had gone straight through the gate into reverse, I spun the wheel back to midships.

"Is she out of gear?" shouted George. "Look out, man. She's going astern."

Hanging on to the headrope, which was again bar taut, I knocked the gear forward into neutral. Working at such

46

slow revolutions, with the shrieking noise of the gulls, it was not easy at first to detect whether the boat was in gear or in neutral.

"Knock her in," shouted George again. "Starboard your wheel; there's another corbal strop coming up; get him inboard."

For a short spell the net came quickly over the roller, which made a sharp, quick, metallic sound as the pawl hit the ratchet. It was easy to foul the net on this ratchet, which would cause holes.

The wind was strong and the night wet and black. There were white caps to the seas which hissed as they raced away into the darkness. My arms were aching, and we had only pulled in a short distance of the first net. Again I felt the full weight of the nets as the headrope slipped a few inches through my hands.

"Knock her in, starboard your wheel," shouted George, and again the pull lessened, the roller clicked fast and more nets and pilchards came aboard. I pulled in another two corbal strops, put the wheel amidships and bent over to knock her out of gear.

At that precise moment there was a sharp bang on the bottom of the boat and the engine stopped.

"We've caught a corbal strop," said George. "Turn up on that headrope quickly."

Once again we found ourselves peering over the stern, but there was little we could do. We cut the strop from the headrope and secured it inboard. We could have started the Kelvin and run her on two cylinders, but I did not know this and George did not suggest (I think rightly) using this engine.

We had no mizzen and no Thornycroft. There were still five and a half nets in the water and the weather was bad and deteriorating fast. I looked over to the north to see if I could spot any of the other boats. But there was nothing to be seen.

"What's the time, George?"

"Just before eleven," he replied. "We must get these nets in, and quickly."

"I can't make any headway without some help from the engine. Shall we try and put the mizzen up?"

We looked at the sail and entangled ropes and decided it was not the answer. I think we had both mentally decided that the sooner we were in and out of it all the better.

"We'll stand in the net-room, one behind the other and pull these nets in," said George.

And this we did for the next hour—while the *Coral* rolled and pitched and the gulls shrieked as if deriding the unbusinesslike manner in which we were working our gear. But it was done and the nets were in, though heaped in a dreadful pile.

The gulls were now quieter, emitting occasional cries as they hovered over the boat before slipping sideways into a long, silent glide. The wind was still increasing and there was a nasty sea running, yet the *Coral*, splendid sea-boat that she was, slipped and slithered over these seas, buoyant as a cork. George primed the Kelvin and she spluttered on two cylinders and then burst into full life on all four.

We switched off the fishing lights and motored under the navigation lights and the small glow of the compass. We steered a northerly course until we had opened up Mevagissey Light. The tide had been on the ebb when we had shot our nets and we had no idea how far to the south we had been set. I thought of the Dodman and particularly the Gwineas, lying somewhere between ourselves and the shore.

The rain affected George's glasses and he had to keep wiping them. I pumped the *Coral* out again and then stood in the engine-room, from where I could lean forward and watch the compass. It was a small box compass and I hoped sincerely that it was reasonably accurate. The tops of the seas were breaking against the *Coral's* starboard side, sending spray clean over the boat, but she sat on the swell of the water and felt wonderfully safe.

We had been running for about thirty minutes when I

48

picked out the Gwineas in my glasses. It looked ugly and dangerous, but I was glad to have seen the rock and George was reassured.

"I can see Chapel Point, George. In ten minutes we should open up Mevagissey Light."

I could now see the white houses on the point and shortly afterwards spotted Mevagissey Light.

"See it, George?" I shouted, and he peered in the direction that I was pointing. It was only just visible to the naked eye through the rain, but through the binoculars the light shone brightly and most welcomingly.

"I've got it," said George and altered course so that the Light remained about twenty degrees off our port bow. We ran on for another fifteen minutes until we were right off the Light, then turned to run in through the harbour mouth. We could see the sea breaking on the harbour wall and the surf at the foot of the great cliffs on either side. We were directly approaching the harbour entrance, lifted up and thrown forward by the following easterly seas, when the disaster suddenly happened.

Our one and only surviving engine stopped. We lay powerless in the grip of the seas.

"Chuck the anchors over, George," I shouted.

"No," he said. "Get hold of that sweep and stand on the nets and we'll try and keep her bow on to the harbour entrance."

But it was useless. I had no purchase with which to use the sweep. As I stood balancing precariously on the nets, staring out over George's head, all I could see was a succession of seas that would either drive us into the harbour or against the wall. Once that had happened, we would never escape in time to avoid breaking up.

Turning, with the full sound of the seas ringing in my ears as they hit the outer harbour walls, I saw to my intense relief that we were going to manage it, for the wind and waves were sweeping us past the Light and into calm waters.

I felt very weak and tired. Neither of us spoke. George took the sweep and slowly sculled the *Coral* past a lugger, whose crew stared at us curiously as they shook the pilchards from their nets. There was just enough water for us to get alongside the southern wall, where we secured the boat and sat down in the stern sheets.

"Let's have a cup of tea," I said and George lit a cigarette.

"Thank you, me dear," he said quietly as I passed him a cup.

We drank our tea in silence and I felt the peace of the harbour. The cottages slept all round us.

"Did you put any paraffin in the Kelvin's tank?" George asked.

"No," I replied, "I didn't."

"Well, she's either got a blocked fuel pipe from the main tank or she's out of paraffin. It's unlikely both her jets would be blocked at the same time."

I took hold of a broom handle and dipped it into the Kelvin's main tank. It was empty. By failing to fill that tank we might easily have lost the boat and our lives.

"Let's get to work," said George, and we never mentioned this incident again.

We unshipped the roller from the starboard side and shipped it across the forward bulkhead of the net-room. Standing on either side of the fish berth, we began to pull the nets over the roller and shake out the pilchards. This was very tiring work and entailed not only keeping the net square in a confined space, but a great deal of arm and wrist movement. In order to free individual pilchards which would not be unmeshed by the more vigorous movements, we would insert our fingers through the meshes around the head of the fish and with a quick flick of the wrist the pilchard would fly clear of the net.

When the fish were more thickly meshed, we would shake the net up and down, smacking it against our oilskin smocks. The movements need to be quick and sure, otherwise, with any quantity of fish, the job would never be finished. But although speed and vigour are essential, a net needs reasonably careful handling, particularly if it is an old one. Otherwise tears begin to appear which will soon develop into large holes if the net is being used a lot.

It took us two and a half hours to clear our six nets of about twenty-seven stone of pilchards. When the last net had been cleared, we replaced the deckboards of the fish-berth so that the pilchards were not exposed to the gulls, and pulled the nets back over the roller into the net-room.

The tide was on the make and the inner harbour was slowly filling. There was just enough water for us to reach our moorings and secure the boat. We took off our oilskins, pumped the *Coral* dry, closed up the engine-room, switched off the fishing light, put on the legs, climbed into the dinghy and went ashore.

With our food-tins under our arms, we walked together up Cliff Walk. We were the last boat in and the last to finish. Below us, the harbour lay shrouded in rain and deserted. I said good night to George and continued up the steep path, past the coastguard station, which had an easterly gale warning up, till I came to our field. Before I left the path I was tempted to look over the wall and down at the breakers far below. I could now feel the full force of the wind and was appalled at the thought that only a few hours back we had been fishing somewhere out in that black void. I remember thinking with dismay of the prospects ahead of us if this night had been a sample of the future.

I walked up the short path and pushed open the porch door. I took off my sea-boots, their black surfaces dotted with pilchard scales, and closed the door against the noise of the gale. I switched on the hall light and glanced at the clock. It was five to four. We had been eleven hours in the *Coral*, I realised. Very tired, I groped my way in darkness up the stairs to bed.

CHAPTER FOUR

Willie Woodbine and
Uncle Dick

It blew hard from the east for twelve days and no boats left the harbour. I was glad when I came down at ten o'clock to a cup of coffee and a late breakfast that it was still blowing a full gale, for I had no inclination to go out again that night.

My hands and fingers were extremely painful, for the net had inflicted little cuts around my nails, and when I had used my hands to wrench the occasional pilchard which refused to be shaken out, I had overcrushed the lifeless body and had consequently been pricked by fish-bones as sharp as needles. Looking now at my hands, I saw that already the fingers looked larger, and I put this down to the constant opening and shutting of the hand as I grasped and pulled the headrope. I later found that this was perfectly true and my fingers became spatulate and my grasp powerful. The palms of my hands grew tough and hard and all the time I was fishing were never free from tar-stains.

George had not yet arrived when I reached the quay, so I sat down on the bench opposite the *Coral* and waited for him. Several fishermen passed and wished me good morning. The sky was leaden and the boats were all at their moorings, safe in the inner harbour. The *Coral* was surging at her chains, while seagulls sat on her forecastle enjoying the motion. She was painted white, and I thought that I would paint her a different colour at Easter.

I looked along the quay to see if I could see George. He was not yet in sight, but Willie Rollins was gently rolling

WILLIE ROLLINS

along in my direction. I watched him as he came. He
walked slowly, but with purpose, making a casual remark
now and then, but not turning his head. I wondered if he
was coming to speak to me, and I was delighted when he
stopped.

"Did you do anything?" he asked, a twinkle in his very
blue eyes.

"Well," I replied, "I believe we caught about four or
five baskets full."

"Have you landed your fish?"

"Not yet. I'm waiting for George," I answered. He
removed his cap and took out a Woodbine.

"Got a light?" he asked. I told him I hadn't, as I didn't
smoke. He went over to one of the others sitting on the
bench; he was handed a box of matches and thrown a remark which I couldn't catch. They all laughed as Willie
Rollins turned his back to the wind and cupped his hands
over the match.

He was known as "Willie Woodbine," and I really believe a proffered Woodbine meant more to him than anything. He used to mend my nets, and he worked a good many hours on them. He would never take any money; he merely growled in a friendly fashion that Woodbines were what he wanted, so I fed him with Woodbines as he worked and rewarded him at the end with a packet or two. It was terribly cheap payment, for mending a net is skilled work and Willie Rollins was an expert.

He tried to teach me how to mend a small hole, but I never mastered the art, though I could just about repair a single mesh or "shank." He would string the net over a line in the loft and discover a great rent, which he would then repair. I would sit and watch him. His eyes were none too good, but he would take out his penknife and with unerring accuracy start to trim and shape the meshes until the hole was the right shape to begin repairing. I never fathomed how he knew exactly when the hole was the correct shape.

He would wind the black cotton round his wooden needle and with a deft movement begin the repair. I watched each mesh grow symmetrically and effortlessly until the hole gradually closed. Now came the part that never ceased to amaze me. The original hole might have been several feet square, but little by little the rent in the net would close until only a small hole was left. He would finish this in a perfect square and then, like a cricketer who had scored a century, he would take off his cap. Here the resemblance to a batsman ceased, for out of the cap he would produce a Woodbine. I would congratulate him and hand him a packet of Woodbines. He had been mending nets for fifty years, but he still seemed to enjoy congratulations.

By now George had joined us.

"Dirty old weather still," he remarked. The fishermen agreed by nods and grunts.

He peered up at me from under his black beret.

"We'll need some baskets," he said and we went over

to the yard under J.B.'s office, where the fish were weighed, cleaned and boxed before being loaded on to lorries and taken to St Austell Station. We took six baskets. A basket of pilchards, filled not quite to the top weighs six stone. There was no need to bring the *Coral* alongside. We could take the baskets out to the boat, fill them up and bring them ashore, all in the dinghy.

George scooped up the pilchards in a pilchard scoop, which resembles a dustpan, but has a longer lip. We filled four and a half baskets.

"Get hold of that bucket and we'll give her a scrub down," said George.

Holding on to the rope's end, I slung the bucket over the side and pulled it up and sloshed the water into the fish-berth while George scrubbed away with a broom. He was quick and workmanlike in his movements and we soon had the fish-pen clean. While I replaced the deckboards and loaded the dinghy with our full baskets, George pumped her out.

"Leave the sixth basket aboard," he called across to me. "It's always useful to have one in the boat."

We cast off the dinghy and sculled her to the steps. Then we carried the baskets up to the weighing machine in the fish store. There we were met by Waller, who weighed the baskets with unbelievable speed, using his hands to scoop up the pilchards from the tops of those baskets weighing over six stone, and throwing them into another basket, which he weighed last. Four and a half baskets of pilchards stood by the weighing machine, totalling twenty-seven stone of fish. They were giving 3s. 3d. a stone for pilchards, so our night's work was worth £4 7s. 9d.

Out of this would have to be taken our petrol and the various shares. It is customary for the owner of the boat to take one share for the boat, one for the nets and one for himself. Some skippers of luggers take a half of the week's taking and then share the rest. We did not go out again this week, so I split this amount with George, after deducting the cost of petrol. I told him that in future I would only take two shares to his one, as I had to learn this fishing business and I would need his help.

I still had a good deal of gear to buy, and these twelve days of bad weather were very useful in this respect. I bought a pram with the name *Babs* written across the stern. As prams go she was well proportioned, broad and sturdy. At this time dinghies and prams were difficult to find and expensive to buy. The *Babs* cost me £20, and J.B. sent one of his lorries to pick her up. We gave her a coat of paint and put her in the water.

I rowed to the outer harbour one afternoon in the *Babs* and started to practise sculling. There was a shallow notch in the stern where I rested the oar. Sitting down facing the stern and holding the oar in both hands, I began to waggle it in a figure-of-eight movement. Almost at once the oar jumped out of the groove. But I kept on practising and after a while I found I could propel and manœuvre the pram. I next tried to scull in a standing position, holding the oar in both hands and looking over the stern of the boat. This I found easier, for the oar tended not to jump out of the groove so readily. Finally, I stood facing the bows and practised sculling with one hand. This was the best way to scull, for standing in the stern left more room in the boat. When I was sufficiently confident I sculled the *Babs* back into the inner harbour and clambered ashore.

On the beach along J.B.'s wall fishermen were still sitting, and it seemed natural and right that they should be. Their life when ashore was unhurried, and they knew how to enjoy their leisure. They were great lovers of conversation and good listeners, but just as content to sit or lean quietly and observantly against the old stone walls. Always, though, whatever the occasion or the discussion, their eyes would turn to the harbour and the sea beyond.

I secured the *Babs*, feeling secretly rather pleased with myself. Not only could I scull, but, still more important, not many people could possibly have seen me practising. But in this I was wrong, for as I turned one of the fishermen rose and came over to me. As he walked I noticed he did not lift his feet much. Around his shoulders hung an old grey sweater with the sleeves tied under his chin. He wore his cap straight, but pulled well over his eyes, so he had to hold back his head slightly in order to see ahead. His face was weather-beaten and with his lower jaw thrust forward he looked not unlike a bulldog. I never saw him hurry and I seldom saw him without his hands in his pockets, yet for all this his conversation had an easy authority which went unquestioned. His name was Willie Barron, but he was known to everyone as Willie Wish. I walked slowly with him along the quayside.

"It takes a bit of practice to scull," he remarked, "but once learnt, never forgotten. You've picked it up quickly." Once more I felt very pleased with myself and murmured something in reply. We walked on a little further until we were opposite Robins's Store. I could see he had something he wanted to tell me.

"You were in the Navy and had your own ship?"

"Yes," I answered.

"The Insurance Agent was asking one or two of us whether you could handle a boat. We told him you could, so you can insure the *Coral* at a fisherman's rate."

I thanked him warmly.

"It's nothing, old son. But look 'ee here, I'd like to see you get another man alongside o' you." He thrust out his jaw still further and nodded his head to emphasise his points. "George Allen's all right, but it would do no harm to ship an extra hand. Three's a better number than two for a boat of the *Coral's* size."

He asked me questions about the other night and shook his head in horror at my answers. I did not want George to take the blame for it all and told Willie that I could at least have filled the tank myself.

"Next time, old man, you stick with the fleet," he said; "and if anything goes wrong there'll be someone there to give you a hand."

57

"Certainly will," I said, and we both agreed it was time for tea.

The following morning I had my first introduction to Uncle Dick. I was in my loft talking with George when the door opened and in came Edgar Husband and his brother, Peter. I probably saw more of these two fishermen than any of the others, because their loft was directly above ours and we were to live near Peter the following winter.

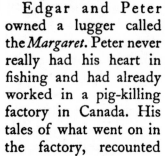

Edgar and Peter owned a lugger called the *Margaret*. Peter never really had his heart in fishing and had already worked in a pig-killing factory in Canada. His tales of what went on in the factory, recounted with a horrifying, good-humoured gusto, made it quite clear that he wanted to return. And eventually he did so. Both brothers had a keen sense of humour, and I spent many hours in their loft, listening to them while they pulled the legs of other members of their crew. They both held themselves well, and Edgar walked with that slight sway from foot to foot so typical of a seaman. His face was full of warm humour and he was generous, sincere, splendid company and nobody's fool.

Now there was a rattle of the latch and they entered our loft; with them came that air of excitement that springs from those who enjoy living. Edgar promptly asked George if he had seen Uncle Dick.

"Not yet," said George; "but I'm just going over."

"Ken here coming?" asked Edgar.

George was nonplussed for a moment, but Edgar continued without waiting for his reply.

"If he's going to be a fisherman he must come and see Uncle Dick."

I had no idea who Uncle Dick was and wondered if I was to endure some unpleasant initiation rite, such as I had been forced to undergo my first week at Liverpool University's School of Architecture.

"The dole," laughed Edgar, realising I was in the dark. "We call the dole Uncle Dick, 6s. 8d. a day if you are married, and you may be in for a couple of weeks. You can't turn down two pounds a week. If the weather's too bad for fishing, you sign your card and collect your money at the end of the week."

So it was that I found myself joining the queue for Uncle Dick, who turned out to be a Mr Richards.

In the evenings Willie Rollins would come up to Beach Road, ask how the Missus was and smoke a Woodbine. He was busy trying to teach me how to mend a small hole and always brought a piece of net with him. When I had gone wrong, a not infrequent occurrence, he would glance across at Biddie and always make the same remark: "Fetch a basket of eggs, Missus, and a big stick." We then gave him a cup of tea, which he would drink with noisy enjoyment. He would ask questions and chuckle to himself a great deal before abruptly announcing that it was time he went. I made a habit of slipping a packet of cigarettes into his hand; I invariably had a supply of Woodbines in store in packets of tens, for he preferred these to twenties, as they fitted more neatly into his cap.

He never thanked me: it would not have been right to show gratitude. The Woodbines were a bond between us. As I walked with him across the green field to the coastguard station, where I bade him good night, I found his silent companionship a soothing nightcap. Biddie would be waiting for my return, and together we would go, look out over the cliff wall and breathe the salt air of the night before going to bed.

The weather was still bad, but George and I had plenty to occupy our time. There were hooks and lines to be bought and made up, wooden tubs to be painted and corks to be cut and fastened to the top edges of the tubs. There were dan buoys to be constructed, and we would need bait-knives, gaffs, grapnels and creepers. For these last three items we went to see the blacksmith.

Albert worked halfway up Polkirt Hill and, like all craftsmen, loved his job. He would mould the metal with strokes as sure and deft and fond as though he were shaping a pat of butter. It was fascinating work to watch. He would place a lump of metal in the fire and turn on the electric fan. In no time at all he would take it out, and golden sparks would fly as the ringing tap of his hammer shaped the metal. He held it up, looked at it, thrust it back in the fire and spoke a few words. Out it would come again, and this time it would be bent over the anvil, tapped gently, held up again to a careful scrutiny. When completely satisfied, the blacksmith would plunge the hot finished article into a bucket of cold water. Albert always had almost more work than he could manage, and he would grumble in a good-natured way that it was all becoming too much for him. Such pressure, if it existed, never showed in his work, which was always first-class.

At the end of the second week in March the weather had fined down sufficiently for the boats to go out again. The unpleasantness of our first night of fishing was no longer fresh in my mind, and I looked forward to shooting the nets and catching more pilchards. We managed ten more days of fishing before March was out and I learnt a lot during this time. In my ignorance I had imagined that fishing took place from about nine o'clock in the morning till some time in the late afternoon. This, of course, was by no means the case, for the bulk of the work, particularly pilchard-driving, was done at night.

When the lining season came round, I was to find that although we pulled the line during the day, we would sometimes leave the harbour at the unspeakable hour of one in the morning.

Our catches varied from fifteen stone to several hauls of

thirty and forty stone. The price for pilchards had dropped to two shillings a stone, at which figure it remained all the time I was fishing. The evenings were growing lighter and we would leave harbour about two hours before nightfall and search for signs. Occasionally we would have information that gannets had been observed, or that boats from Polperro or Looe had been having good catches. But very often there would be few signs, if any, and after cruising around the boats would shoot their nets and hope that they had chosen a lucky spot.

During this searching period we would often pass close to a lugger and they would wave and shout a greeting. I could see the man in the wheelhouse, with his head and shoulders framed in the open window, gazing intently ahead, as he leaned against the wheel. There would be one leaning against the mizzen mast, watching out astern, while the other two would be standing in the net-room, also watching the sea and sky. Abruptly one of these would disappear down the forecastle to inspect the galley fire.

"Might as well shoot here," George would say after we had been circling around watching the sky and the movements of the other boats. We then shut down the Kelvin and left the Handy Billy idling in neutral; and away the nets would go. I shot the headrope a few times and gradually acquired the knack of using the engine to keep the headrope taut.

On a calm night, when the nets were all out and both engines silent, I was strongly aware of the deep peace around us, and we would eat our food leaning comfortably against the boat's side, and gaze across the dark water to the coast. Gradually the night would close down and across the water the masthead lamps of the boats would burn more brightly. Lulled by the movement of the boat, we drank our tea, and watched the lights ashore go out. Faintly we would hear the last train down from the north and watch it slowly crawl like a yellow caterpillar through the darkness.

Sometimes we would shoot the nets twice, and this was

tiring work. The fish were not there in quantity, and at this time of year they were thin in quality compared with the winter pilchards. At other times we would haul in a few corbal strops to see if any fish were going in, and if they were we might decide to leave the nets in the water a good deal longer. If there was a moon the fish usually would not go to net until it had set.

I found these long evenings most pleasant. Sometimes Biddie would accompany us, which always amused the fishermen. On a still night the crew of the *Margaret* would hail us and Edgar Husband's voice would ring across the water: "Is the missus aboard?" The fishermen insisted that Biddie brought us luck, and strangely enough, we always did seem to do better when she was out with us. She loved these occasions, but when we were lying to the nets, she found the motion of the boat uncomfortable. However, provided she did not bend down to tend the primus and kept up in the bows, clear of the smell of the bilges and engine, she was quite all right.

We had hand-lines in the boat and we would all three fish off the bottom while George talked of the hazards to bear in mind when netting. He would speak of the times when the fish teem in their thousands; at such times great care must be taken not to leave the nets in the water too long. If a solid white wall of fish should hit the nets, the sheer weight will pull them to the bottom of the sea. Nothing can be done to save the fleet of nets.

It needs little imagination to visualise the drama that follows. The crew, full of spirits at the prospect of a big haul, eagerly shoot their nets, while around them scores of gannets plummet down to the dark waters. Close by the black hump of a whale breaks the surface and with a snort blows water into the air. Ten nets are out when the owner decides not to shoot any more. Two of the crew go down for a cup of tea, but the owner and the other hand remain on deck watching the nets. Even as they watch, the white buffs and the corbal strops near the boat begin to bob

63

and duck in the water. With a shout to the two men below, the headrope is cast off and in a trice the nets are manned, for the crew is now fully alive to the danger.

The first piece of net comes over the roller white with fish and fearfully heavy. There is desperation on the men's faces as they lie back and pull with all their strength. But there is nothing they can do, for the nets, solid with fish, are leading down into the waters; a broad path of silver fish disappearing towards the bottom of the sea until the whole length of net is up and down, leading direct from the boat's side to the bottom of the sea. The climax to the drama is reached when the captain takes a knife and severs the head-rope. His nets are gone, his catch has gone; and all in a matter of minutes. The engines are started and the lugger heads for home. Down in the cuddy tea is brewed and little is said. It has happened before and will happen again; philosophically, it is accepted and there's an end of the matter.

I learnt of the menace of the dogfish which attacks the ensnared pilchards with savage ferocity. On these occasions the dogfish swarm on the nets in such numbers that it is difficult to pull the nets aboard. The last net they will attack in frenzy until there is nothing left but the headrope. So vicious is their attack on this remaining net that they will even bite the cork corbal strops.

The nets are always completely ruined, and often the fishermen are unable to go to sea for weeks, owing to their hands being cruelly spurred by dogfish. I heard of the sad spectacle of gannets diving on the nets and drowning in their meshes.

Sometimes the net is "knocked up" by masses of swimming pilchards. When this happens, it lies on the top of the water, a great attraction for the gannets. Folding their long black-tipped wings, the birds will dive to their death. For though their dives will take them clean through the net, they will find it difficult to regain the surface—for as the pilchards die so the net will sink, taking the gannets down and drowning them.

I gathered that whales were common and sharks sometimes got into the nets and did enormous damage. I was
amazed to hear that when the fish were prolific they could
be smelt by a man on the bows, for on the water appeared
great oily splats which gave off a distinct fishy smell. The
fishermen would watch the water closely for these signs.
Sometimes at night by banging a 56-lb. weight on the boat's
deck fish could be started; you then watched them racing
away from the bows. Of all this George Allen would talk
easily and fluently until it was time to pull our nets.

As the nights were fine, we shook the fish out as we pulled
the nets aboard. It was slow work, but I didn't catch any
more corbal strops around the propeller. Indeed, I was
beginning to find that rhythm and right mental approach so
necessary for this kind of work. A net and a pilchard were
no longer unfamiliar objects, and I began to feel and also, I
believe, look a little more like a fisherman. We would usually
be finished between two and three in the morning, though
sometimes when we shot the nets twice, it would be later.

One evening George suggested we should ship another
hand, Sam Ingrouille. Sam knew nothing about fishing.
He had spent twenty-three years of his life in the Royal
Navy, had ended up as a Chief Petty Officer and was now
wanting a job to augment his pension. A Channel Islander
himself, he had married a Mevagissey girl and lived at the
western end of our road.

I went to see him and liked him at once. He was very
tall and thin and gave a deep impression of honesty and
dependability. I asked him if he would come with us, and
he said he would.

"Fine. Can you come along tonight?" I asked him.

"Yes," he said, and so Sam joined us.

Shortly after Sam's arrival I bought another three nets,
so that we now had nine in the boat. The weather was
excellent and we fished all through April, but not with a
great deal of success, for the fishing was thin. When our
night's work was done we would walk along the quay and

split up and make our way home. Sometimes I would stop and lean over the wall and look down at the harbour, where a few crews were still shaking out their fish.

On one such night I heard a great deal of excited chattering coming from the crew of a lugger, so I stopped and watched them as they moored their boat. I knew by now that this was the crew of the *Pride of the West*, renowned for their talking, and led by Albert, who talked faster than any person I have ever met, often repeating a phrase several times before going on to the next part of his sentence.

At sea on a calm night their ceaseless chatter could be heard across the water, and when it reached a real crescendo of noise we all knew that they were discussing whether or not to shoot their nets. Then when silence reigned we knew they were of one accord and the nets were about to be shot. After which they would retire below deck to carry on their conversation in the confined space of the forecastle. I cannot imagine what it sounded like down there.

So peace would reign on the water and nothing more would be heard for a considerable time, and then suddenly the chattering would begin all over again. This new outburst signified that a lively discussion was being held as to whether or not the nets should be hauled.

On one occasion, the *Pride of the West* was approaching the outer harbour and an excessively keen discussion was in progress as to whether there was sufficient water in the inner harbour for them to get alongside and off-load their fish. The whole crew, including the helmsman, was gesticulating and talking at tremendous speed and with great vigour, when suddenly, just as the *Pride of the West* was entering the outer harbour, the neglected tiller swung over and jammed under a fish-box. In a second the boat had swung hard a-port. For one moment there was a horrified silence aboard the lugger, then with a horrible crash the *Pride of the West* hit the harbour wall a full-blooded blow with her bows. If their chatter had been considerable before, it now reached unprecedented heights.

66

However, all was well, and when next morning we gathered round to see what damage had been done to the *Pride of the West*, Albert and his crew were in great form, patting the old boat's hull and showing us proudly that no real damage had been done, though it would be necessary to scarf a piece on to her stem.

They were a splendid crew, and as I now watched them climb over the boat's side and down into their dinghy, their chatter never ceased. Up on to the quay they climbed and there they stood in a little group with Albert in the middle, all talking and nodding as hard as ever. A happy crew, the *Pride of the West*, and I left them, feeling the happier for having watched them.

Towards the end of April we decided to take the nets ashore and give the boat a good clean-up and a coat of paint. We had not yet finished making up our spilter line, but our dog lines were ready. During this period I had one or two altercations with George which eventually led to our parting for the summer. As things turned out, it was to his advantage as well as mine, for he missed an appalling summer's fishing and I was taught lining by one of the best fishermen in Mevagissey. George joined me again the next winter, and by that time I had learnt much and had gained sufficient experience to give the orders when they were necessary. But I always liked the three of us to decide together as far as possible when and where we should shoot our gear.

Sam and I beached the *Coral* on the little shelving sandy beach in the outer harbour, and, listing her over, scrubbed underneath her with brushes and sand before giving a coat of red lead to her keel and bottom planks. We had to do this on successive days, as only one side could be painted at a time, but the rest of the *Coral's* spring painting could be done at her moorings.

Biddie helped in the painting, but not on the hull. She was given the job of red-leading the deck-boards, which she did well; if it was uneven at times, it did not matter.

At any rate, it certainly amused the fishermen, who would remark to me that the missus was making a proper job. We painted the *Coral* blue-green, and inside we painted her white. With her red-brown decks and her newly painted hull, she looked handsome.

Easter was approaching and visitors were wandering along the quayside in the warm spring air. It felt as though summer was just round the corner and there was excitement in the air. But two problems were looming up which had to be faced. The first problem concerned accommodation. Mr and Mrs Church had originally warned us that we would have to leave at the end of May, as they always let the house during the summer months. We had searched hard for a place for some time, but without success. Mary Husband temporarily came to our rescue and said she would take us in for a couple of weeks, but after that we had nowhere to go.

We were beginning to be rather concerned about this housing problem, when one day we found a note thrust through our letter-box, telling us to telephone a certain Mevagissey number. We did so at once and were told, to our great surprise, that we could have a flat for the whole summer at a most reasonable figure. It turned out to be just what we wanted, with a garden and plenty of room. We were both delighted, and examined the note. There was no signature, no address, and we never found out who did us this good turn, though we made many enquiries.

Our second problem worried me a great deal. Neither Sam nor I was capable of fishing with long lines. I needed, as Willie Wish had told me, a top-grade fisherman and no top-grade fisherman was going to jump at joining a boat with two complete novices aboard. I knew that some of the fishermen were discussing my problem and, in spite of my very real concern for our future, I was sustained by this fact and Biddie's quiet assurance that something would turn up.

There was little that I could do but wait and see what

68

would happen. Had I taken some form of action to counter our problem, I do not believe I would have succeeded. This was one of those moments of passive acceptance when the water is deep and the way not clear. It is as important to recognise these periods as to appreciate the moment for decisive action. So I waited. I knew that Willie Rollins, Willie Wish, Peter Barron and the Husbands had our interests at heart.

Then one day our problem was solved. It was Willie Rollins who came up one evening to break the news to us.

"George Pearce will go with you," he said without any preamble, and I very gratefully gave him the usual packet of Woodbines, which promptly disappeared into his cap. We were all three delighted and Biddie poured out cups of tea.

Later, when I walked with Willie across the field, he intimated that it would be wise to give George Pearce half my boat's share, for he was, as Willie put it, a really good man. I had little doubt that Willie and others had engineered this for me, and I felt a great warmth for him as I watched his small figure, with its rolling gait, go steadily down past the coastguard station to the harbour below.

On the way back I called in at Sam's house and told him the good news. I was taken into his warm kitchen and given yet another cup of tea and an excellent piece of home-made sponge cake.

That night Biddie and I went to bed easy of mind, for our two problems had been solved. We now had somewhere to live for the coming summer and, still more important, a top-grade fisherman had agreed to join us as crew and to show us lining.

CHAPTER FIVE

George Pearce

As he leant comfortably against the wall, he appeared to me a veritable Falstaff in the flesh, a great Humpty-Dumpty of a man, on whose bull-like shoulders sat a round head, and to whose ample paunch clung a long grey sweater. His cap was flat and sat slightly to the back of his head. His eyes were a quizzical blue and shrewd, and he chewed a plug of tobacco continuously, turning his head occasionally to let out a stream of spittle.

It was with distinct apprehension that I now approached George Pearce. I had a suspicion that he was a man of few words.

"I hear you would like to come with us, George," I ventured. It was, however, as I had feared, for he looked at me and said nothing, and there resulted one of those awkward pauses in which the lead has to be firmly taken and something has to be said. It was clear that George was in no way embarrassed; so I began again:

"I'd be very grateful if you *would* come along with us."

This made a sharper impression. He turned to spit and murmured something I could not catch. I suggested he might like to come and see our gear, and added that the loft would be open all morning. But I received only a curt nod, followed by another stream of spittle, in the face of which I beat as dignified a retreat as I could muster.

Once I had gained the sanctuary of my loft I sat down on a wooden box and, looking through the windows down into J.B.'s yard, gave a deep sigh of despair. The meeting with George Pearce could not have been more awkward, and I

GEORGE PEARCE

began to wonder whether I had not made a great mistake in parting from George Allen. Sitting thus wrapped in increasing gloom, I was suddenly startled by the abrupt entrance of Edgar Husband. At once I felt better.

"George Pearce is a very good man," he remarked immediately. "He'll put you right and he knows what he's about."

I was grateful indeed for this news, and told Edgar that

after my first conversation with George Pearce I was beginning to wonder whether something had gone wrong; perhaps George had never had any real intention of coming with us. At this Edgar laughed aloud, and no sound could have been more reassuring.

"Of course he's coming with you, and you've got a damn' good man in George," he assured me.

Edgar had a habit of screwing up his eyes when he laughed. He had the most infectious laugh and the most comical expression I have ever known. Then suddenly, speaking very quickly and with a perfectly straight face, he would make some preposterous statement. But it would be too much for him and he would screw up his eyes again and laugh silently till the tears ran down his cheeks. Edgar and Peter Husband were great leg-pullers, though there was never any malice in their fun. I had many laughs with them and they were obviously fascinated by the *Coral's* activities.

We both went over to see Uncle Dick, and on the way back I popped into Roland Billins's to have a cup of coffee and a crab sandwich. Apart from the fact that his crab sandwiches were quite excellent, I enjoyed having a yarn with Roland about football. He kept goal for St Austell and Cornwall and was no mean performer. There was talk of Mevagissey having a football team next season, and I told him I would very much like to play for the side.

I left Roland Billins and went outside, past a group of fishermen standing around Williams's shop, round the corner and along the quay to my loft. When I arrived I found the door open and George Pearce examining my gear.

"Got to get these dog lines made up," he grunted and, turning his head, emitted a stream of tobacco juice which hit the floor with a splash. I wasn't sure what he had said so gave a noncommittal answer, which seemed to satisfy him. George Pearce was never easy to hear or understand, for he always chewed tobacco and hardly opened his mouth when he spoke. It irritated him when I asked him to repeat himself, so until I got the hang of things I was constantly misunderstanding him and doing the opposite of what he intended.

That afternoon we finished making up the dog lines, which carried some 2,700 hooks, each of us working 900 hooks. The usual number worked by each member of a crew is 1,000 hooks. But George had rightly considered that 1,000 hooks each would be more than either Sam or I could manage. After we had finished and locked the loft door, I went into J.B.'s office and ordered six stone of pilchards for baiting the line the following day.

"Going to put your dog line aboard?" he enquired.

"Yes," I replied. "And George Pearce is coming with us."

He smiled, and I could tell he was pleased that George Pearce was going to ship along with us. I said good night to J.B. and walked home. It was pleasant to sit tired and relaxed after supper watching the light slowly fade over Chapel Point. Next week we would no longer be sitting here in the evenings, for our time was up and we were moving down into the village to live with Mary Husband for ten days before going to our new home. We were going to miss this lovely view, but there were other things which would, in one way or another, compensate for this. At our present home we had no bathroom, but had to make do with a tin tub which we filled with kettles and in which we washed before our sitting-room fire. Mrs Church had been very friendly. Her husband was a remarkable old man, well into his seventies, who every morning of the year, irrespective of wind and rain, would go down the wild, steep cliff path to the beach below and collect firewood. Sometimes he did not collect much, but he never failed to bring back something. Biddie won his admiration by bathing in the early morning, but I did not attempt to compete. Three years in the Mediterranean had completely ruined what pleasure I had ever taken in bathing around these shores.

73

The following morning we collected our six stone of pilchards and salt, and began to cut up the bait. Each pilchard was cut into five or six pieces, and these were then swept with the blade of the knife into a box containing salt. Periodically we would sharpen the bait-knives on a carborundum. My first attempt at cutting up a pilchard produced an angry snort from George Pearce.

"They'll be bloody strawberry jam before you've finished."

I could see his point and, glancing across at Sam's efforts, saw the same applied to him. I had been sawing through the fish rather as though I had been cutting a slice of bread. I watched George deftly cut up half a dozen pilchards and realised that the secret lay in cutting in one motion and not sawing backwards and forwards. I tried again and met with immediate success. Sam too had got the hang of it and in no time we had our bait cut up and salted.

George next showed us how to set up the tubs of line preparatory to baiting them. First and foremost they must be at a convenient height so that one does not have to bend. We had some nine tubs, and in each was a length of line which had, at regular three-foot intervals, fourteen-inch "stops" or lengths of thin line, to the end of which were attached the hooks. The tub containing the line would then be placed alongside an empty tub with a box of bait lying between them. Always, when the first piece of line was put into the empty tub, a short length, free of hooks, was left hanging over the edge so that all the tubs of line could eventually be joined up. The actual baiting up of the line consisted of taking the hook out of the cork, fixing on the piece of bait and placing the baited hook inside the perimeter of the adjacent empty tub with the line coiled down in the centre.

Thus, when the baiting-up was finished, around tea-time, we had all nine tubs of line baited, with the 300 baits in each tub neatly stacked one on top of the other and the line coiled in the centre all ready for shooting. All they now needed was to be connected up to make the one long line.

74

The hooks were a good two inches in the shank and the bait had to be fixed firmly, otherwise it would drop off. To prevent this, the hook was passed once through the piece of bait, then with a quick twist passed through it again.

We carried the tubs down to the *Babs* and sculled her out to the *Coral*. There we covered the line with an old tarpaulin. This was most important, for the seagulls would have gone for the baits. Even so, it was not an uncommon sight to see a gull caught on a hook, having managed to get under a tarpaulin. In such distressing cases the hook would be taken from the bird's beak—no easy operation—and the creature would fly off, apparently in no discomfort.

We took aboard our two dan buoys and flags, two gaffs, eighty fathoms of dan line in a basket and our two grapnels. Finally, we ordered six stone of bait and a box of salt to be ready the following morning.

"Engines all right?" George enquired.

"I think so. I've topped up all three tanks and we've five gallons of petrol and five gallons of paraffin to spare. What time shall we start, George?"

"Be down at five," he answered, and with that we parted. Sam walked home with me, for it was not much further for him to come up the cliff path.

"Well, Sam," I said as we reached Beach Road, "we shall know what we are in for tomorrow."

"True enough," he replied. "And so will George," he added shrewdly.

We both laughed aloud, though I can't think why, for neither of us had ever pulled a line in our life, nor handled fish. The number of fish that I had caught on a hook could be counted on one hand, and the tricky business of taking them off the hook had been shelved whenever possible. When this had not been possible, I had taken minutes grabbing at the squirming fish in a most unprofessional manner. It now suddenly occurred to me that 2,700 hooks were going to lie on the bottom of the sea. If only a ninth of the hooks were taken by fish, somebody had to free 300 fish of all types and shapes. George had a big responsibility.

"See you at five," I called after Sam as he walked to the end of Beach Road where he lived.

After a supper of fresh fish followed by fruit and Cornish cream, Willie came up to see how things were going. We talked for an hour and then, as usual, he suddenly got up to go. I walked with him across the field.

"It's bad luck to wish you good luck," he said as we parted. I knew what he meant and that it would be tempting Providence to say any more.

This was one of the superstitions that always intrigued me. I had my own theory about this particular belief that one must never wish another fisherman good luck before he goes out.

By doing so I think it is felt that the game is given away and the fish know one is coming. Far better that no reference is made to the possibilities of a fine catch. Let it simply be a question of men going out to sea in their boats with no ulterior motives. Anyone who has worked with a fishing fleet will have noticed this apparent unconcern and the detached attitude of fishermen before going aboard. But beneath this light-hearted approach, there is also a determination that is not apparent to the uninitiated.

The alarm went off at four-twenty. It was dark and cold, and I was loth to leave our feather mattress. I dressed quickly as Biddie made up a thermos flask of coffee; my sandwiches had already been made the previous evening. We both had a cup of tea and I had a boiled egg. It was a quarter to five and time I went.

"Good luck," she said.

"Good thing Willie can't hear us," I replied and kissed her goodbye.

As I reached the harbour, I could see cottage lights shining wanly in the first grey light of morning. Figures were moving around the quay, engines were spluttering to life and several dinghies were being sculled out to the boats lying at their moorings. Sam and I arrived simultaneously, to be joined shortly by George. We had already collected the basket of bait and a box of salt from J.B.'s store. We all three climbed aboard the *Babs* and, standing in the stern, I sculled her the short distance to the *Coral*. Sam stowed our food packets up forward while I opened up the engine-room and switched on the petrol, primed the Thornycroft and swung her. She started easily and I closed the hissing priming valves.

"Go astern," shouted George as he cast off our moorings. "Starboard your helm."

I put the wheel over to starboard.

"Starboard your helm," shouted George again and, moving with surprising speed and agility across the net-room, he spun the wheel viciously to port. I was bewildered and thankful when George took the wheel, while I went down to start the Kelvin. The engine started easily and I glanced over the side to watch the even flow of her exhaust, an indication that the engine was firing on all four cylinders.

Starboard your helm, port your helm; what the hell was George talking about? I thought. And then it suddenly dawned on me. When he had shouted at me to starboard my helm, he was thinking of the tiller, and if the tiller is put over to starboard the boat's bows will swing to port; if, however, one puts the wheel to starboard, the boat's bows will swing to starboard. George's order had been "Starboard your helm," but the *Coral* had no helm, but a wheel, and I had naturally put her wheel to starboard. Obviously then, in future, if he ever mentioned "helm" when giving a wheel order, I must put the wheel in the opposite direction. "Starboard your helm" meant put the wheel over to port. I was still thinking this over when I heard a ghastly roaring noise.

Glancing up, I saw George being violently sick over the boat's side. When he had finished he seized his cap in his right hand, rubbed it vigorously around his face and put it back on his head. Sam had heard the noise too and turned just in time to see this extraordinary spectacle. I caught his eye, but he was obviously as bewildered as I was and turned round quickly. I thought I'd better say something.

"Sorry you're not feeling too well, George." He turned and gave me a withering glance. He couldn't have looked more healthy as he took out his knife and cut himself a *fresh plug of tobacco. He had consumed a quantity of beer* the night before.

So began our first day of dogging. As we cleared Chapel Point the night was fast disappearing, and as George hauled off to the south, the Gwineas and the Dodman stood out clearly in the early morning light. I suddenly remembered I hadn't switched the Kelvin over to paraffin, and quickly opened the paraffin fuel tap and closed the petrol feed.

Standing in the engine-room hatch, I watched first the Gwineas and then the Dodman come abreast. Looking at them, I thought again of that first night out and realised how lucky we had been. Eighteen miles ahead of us lay the Manacles, a dangerous cluster of rocks, while off our starboard bow the wedgelike shape of the Gull Rock could be seen against the background of the coast. Over to port several luggers were heading in the same direction as ourselves; amongst them I recognised Edgar's boat, the *Margaret.*

Sam, who had already joined up the tubs of line and bent on the two grapnels to both the dan lines, had now begun cutting up the basket of bait. Satisfied that the engines were running smoothly, I went forward and joined him. While George steered, Sam and I cut up the six stone of pilchards, an operation which had to be performed right under the eyes of George Pearce. But after five minutes it was obviously clear that he was satisfied with our efforts, for he no longer paid us any attention. In half an hour we had finished cutting up the pilchards and I returned to take up my customary position in the engine-room hatchway. From there I could easily reach the wheel, though there was no need with George there, and attend quickly to the engines when necessary.

I glanced at George Pearce as he stood in front of me at the side of the *Coral's* small wheel, a massive, squat figure with great, bunched shoulders and thick neck. He spat over the side periodically, but said nothing, keeping his eyes fixed ahead of the boat's bows. After a while he took out his pipe and lit it. I was not sure what had happened to the tobacco he had been chewing; presumably it had dissolved. Up forward Sam leaned on the *Coral's* forecastle, watching the coast. I thought I'd join him again and, squeezing past George, climbed over the net-room, across the fish-berth and into the forepart of the boat, where stood our two dan buoys with their yellow flags flapping in the wind.

"All right, Sam?" I enquired.

"Fine. How's George?" he added with a sly smile as he began to roll a cigarette.

"He seems to have recovered from his morning sickness," and we laughed. But not for long. At that moment the Kelvin began to miss on two of her cylinders.

"Engine," shouted George before I had time to turn round.

"Oh Lor'," muttered Sam as I clambered aft.

I smiled sweetly at George as I squeezed past him, trying to give the appearance that I was in no way concerned. He glared at me as though the missing cylinders were my fault and I had done it on purpose. I disappeared quickly into the engine-room. It was hot and noisy as I leant in the confined space and groped with an adjustable spanner to undo the forward carburettor jet. I got it loose and unscrewed it with the fingers of my left hand. It came away with a spurt of petrol which ran down into the bilges. Still holding the jet, I tried to switch off the petrol feed to the carburettor. I succeeded in doing this, but also in dropping the jet into the bilges.

"Got it?" came a roar from above and, looking up from

79

my kneeling position, I saw the great round face of George glaring down at me.

"Nearly," I lied weakly.

"Well, is it blocked, man? Is it blocked?" Fortunately, before I had to confess I had lost the wretched thing, he had disappeared.

Praying hard, for the chances of finding the jet were small, I again groped round the side of the engine and plunged my hand down into the bilges as far as I could go. There were plenty of pilchard scales and fish-hooks and suddenly I felt something small and hard. It was the jet all right and I breathed a great sigh of relief.

I stood up, stiff from the awkward position in which I had been working. "Here we are, George."

He took the jet, held it up to his eye, then put it to his mouth and blew a great blast of air through the tiny aperture. Without a word, but with a keen glance, he handed it back to me. I put it back, screwed it up with a spanner and switched on the petrol. Coming up again, I wiped my hands on some engine-room waste and, leaning over the side, watched the intermittent splash of the exhaust quicken to an even flow as the forward two cylinders of the engine fired.

Sam had been watching from his distant and enviable position up forward and gave the thumbs-up sign. George glanced round, gave a slight nod, took his pipe from his mouth and spat. That slight nod from George delighted me, and I thought I had detected a momentary flash of amusement in those shrewd blue eyes.

By now we were outside the Manacles and slightly to the south of them. George had been altering course a good deal, glancing frequently at the coast till he had got his bearings and was in the position from which he wished to shoot the line.

"Switch off the Kelvin," he ordered, and while I was doing this he leant over into the engine-room and throttled down the Thornycroft. At the same time he called to Sam to pass a dan buoy. Swiftly he bent on the eighty fathoms of dan line, then, with a quick glance astern at the coast and at the compass, he lifted the dan buoy over the side and shouted to me to go ahead. As the *Coral* gently gathered way, with a flinging motion of his right arm, he shot the dan line in a flat arc from out of the basket.

"Knock her out," he shouted and at the same time he flung the basket up into the bows and dragged the first tub of line towards him across the net-room. George was now holding the grapnel and when Sam had got the rest of the tubs set up to his liking, George lowered the grapnel, on to whose flukes the long line was attached and the shooting of the dog line began.

"Knock her in," cried George, as he sent arc after arc of line with baited hooks flying through the air.

"Knock her out," he shouted as the boat gathered too much way, and, glancing quickly at the compass and then round at the dan buoy lying now some distance astern, he continued this rhythmic movement, not unlike a man sowing seed. One, two, three tubs of line had already gone and the dan buoy lay well astern. In the fourth tub the line fouled and quickly stopping the engine, I watched George hold the quivering line tight, and with incredible speed and certainty of movement free the fouled hooks and continue shooting. Should anything go wrong and the line begin to take charge, there were always two bait knives conveniently placed and ready for immediate use.

I watched very closely and tried to anticipate when to go ahead and when to stop the engine. Generally I was able to forestall a good many of George's orders. At the end of thirty minutes he shot overboard the last piece of the dog line and threw over the second grapnel, to which the end of the line was attached. Then it was easy going and in no time the other eighty fathoms of dan line had snaked out of the basket. Finally, George lifted the second dan buoy and dropped it on to the water. We watched it as it drifted slowly astern. The whole length of line now lay underneath

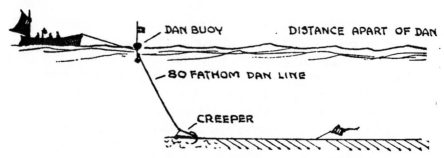

these two marker buoys, anchored on the bottom of the sea by the two grapnels.

We turned the *Coral* round and motored slowly back to the first dan buoy, which we could just see bobbing up and down, a yellow speck in the distance. We all got out our food packets. The time was nearly nine o'clock. I ate with enjoyment and drank my hot coffee and wondered what Biddie was doing. Then I thought of the mile and a half of line and the 2,700 hooks lying on the bottom between the two grapnels, and I wondered what was happening down there and what the bottom was like. I asked George about this and he told me that it was rocky in places, a good bit of ground.

"There's the *Margaret* beginning to get their line," and he pointed over our starboard bow. I asked George how many hooks the *Margaret* worked.

"Six thousand," and he smiled knowingly as he cut another plug of tobacco, which he promptly put into his mouth. By now we had reached the eastern dan, the one we had launched first. George had donned his oilskin smock and hoisted the mizzen. Sam had put on his black naval oilskin, but there was no need for me to follow suit, since I had to tend to the engine, mizzen and wheel in order to keep the *Coral* up to the line. George was going to pull the line while Sam stood alongside him and coiled the line down into the first tub. As soon as a tub was full of line again, Sam would unknot the line and George alone would pull and coil the line into the next empty tub, while Sam *from now on would spend his whole time baiting-up.*

82

BUOYS FROM TWO TO SEVEN MILES   DAN BUOY

LINE WITH HOOKS
RESTING ON SEABED   DOG LINE   CREEPER

We approached the dan buoy and, leaning over, George hoisted it aboard. The operations of getting the line had begun. The time was nine-twenty. Pulling the dan rope in at great speed and at the same time coiling it into his right hand, George neatly flung the coils into the basket. In no time the dan rope was up and down, and, putting the line across his great shoulders, he broke the grapnel out of the ground.

"Go ahead," he called as the rest of the dan line came quickly aboard. Looking down into the water, I could see dozens of vague green shapes lying apparently unattached to the line as it disappeared at a steep slant into deep dark water. It was most exciting and I could feel that George was watching me closely. I glanced at him quickly, and although he appeared unimpressed, I had a feeling he was as pleased as we were.

Hand over hand he pulled the line, till the first dogfish came aboard. I saw the fish sent spinning with astonishing ease into the net-room, which we were using as a fish-hatch. There had been no jerk or sign of effort as George had removed the fish. I watched closely as he handled fish after fish with the same effortless skill. It was fascinating work to watch and a little frightening to think that I would soon have to pull the line and handle the fish myself.

Suddenly George stopped hauling and, with a dogfish in his hand, showed me how to hold the creature.

"See that spur," he said. "Unless you hold him by the back of the head, he'll prick you with it and then you'll know about it."

I watched him as in his right hand he grasped each dog-fish by the back of its flat head and, giving both the fish and the hook a quick twist, dispatched the fish by a flick of the wrist into the hold below. These dogfish with their cruel green eyes, greyish-white streamlined bodies and under-slung mouths, were exactly like sharks. They paid us two shillings a stone for them and they were sold in fish-shops as rock salmon.

The weather was fine and sunny with a fresh wind blowing from the north.

"Starboard your helm," shouted George and forgetting that I should put the wheel over to port if he mentioned the word "helm," I spun the little wheel to starboard.

"Starboard, starboard your bloody helm," shouted George again.

Quickly I spun the wheel back to port, but it suddenly jammed as one of the wires had taken a riding turn. Fever-ishly I cleared this.

"Knock her out, man," cried George, for by now we had ridden over the line which was leading under the boat and the slanting line of fish could be seen on our port side.

"Ease your sheet." Gradually the *Coral's* bows came round.

"Port your helm." Keeping my head, I at once put the wheel to starboard.

"Go ahead." And once again George began the long, tiring job of pulling the line. He glanced at the mizzen.

"Haul in on your sheet. Knock her out," and he stared at me long and hard.

I was beginning to feel tired, for it was all new to me and, apart from the physical effort of moving quickly to tend to the wheel, engine and mizzen, there was the mental anxiety of trying to keep the boat up to the line so that George's task was no harder than it need be. I envied Sam, who stood calmly coiling the line down after George had cleared it of fish. But it wasn't long before George told Sam to start and bait up a line. Slowly and methodically, Sam began to set

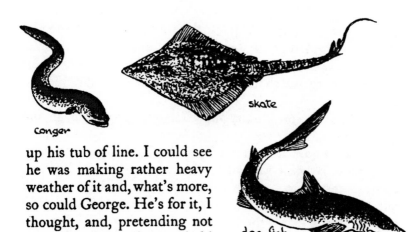

conger

skate

dog-fish

up his tub of line. I could see he was making rather heavy weather of it and, what's more, so could George. He's for it, I thought, and, pretending not to notice, I saw George hold on to the line with one hand, heard him growl at Sam as he rearranged Sam's tub and bait-box in a much better position. I couldn't help smiling— a smile which quickly disappeared as George called out again those three words I was to hear so often.

"Knock her in."

And so it went on for five hours, knock her in, knock her out, ease your sheet, take in your sheet, starboard your helm, port your helm, ease your helm—until I wondered how much longer I could keep going. Once, when I was fumbling with the mizzen sheet, I heard an ugly roar, and on turning saw to my horror that Sam had been handed the line to hold so that George could come to my aid. In spite of his great bulk, he was across the net-room in a trice, had settled the sheet to his liking and was back in his place pulling the line towards the eastern dan buoy with the same steady skill and rhythm.

We caught three huge skates which could be felt and seen when they went broadside on to the line as heavy great green triangular shapes. They were gaffed and dragged aboard, and as they lay moving ponderously on the hatches, they emitted a hissing noise. We caught several rays and two turbot and finally a great 80 lb. conger, thick as a man's thigh. We gaffed this vicious great fish and made no attempt

85

to take out the hook. A quick slash with the bait-knife and the fish wriggled across the net-room and dropped into the hold. George said never a word, but Sam paused in his baiting up to watch this huge fish before it disappeared below.

"He'd give you a nasty nip, George," said Sam, giving me a wink.

"You'd know about it all right," said George with a bit of a smile. By now we had reached the end of the line and Sam, in answer to George's enquiry to know the time, took out his watch. It was half-past two in the afternoon. The grapnel was aboard, the dan rope was being hauled in fast and here was the eastern dan buoy itself with its yellow flag drumming in the fresh wind. George lifted it aboard and the whole line was in, shot and hauled in just over five hours. I had already started up the Kelvin and, now taking the wheel, headed the *Coral* up-Channel for the Dodman. There was a strong wind blowing from the north and a choppy sea into which we had to punch our way home. At once a stinging sheet of spray went over the boat. George was well protected, but Sam got the brunt of it down his neck. Both engines were full ahead and I left them there, for there was no reason to reduce speed.

In spite of the fact that George had been standing pulling the line for the best part of five hours and had handled approximately a thousand fish, he wasted no time in setting up a tub of line and beginning the tedious baiting-up process, which had to be completed that night ready for the following morning.

I stood in the stern steering and baiting-up my line, while Sam and George, standing alongside each other in the fish berth, with their tubs on the hatch coverings of the net-room, baited up their lines facing me. Sam was a slow, methodical worker and I could see he would never go much faster. His movements were deliberate, and to every one hook that he baited, George did two. They could not have looked more different as they stood there baiting their lines.

86

George was squat and massive in his yellow, faded oilskin, with a bit of a scarf wrapped round his neck, while Sam was tall and lean, over six feet two inches, with a grey trilby pulled well down over his angular face, his body protected by a black naval oilskin. Sam looked very, very tired and the back of his neck must have been sore from the stinging spray. It didn't affect me so much, for George was in front of me and provided a nice spot of shelter. Periodically an extra large crash of the boat's bows into these head seas would be followed by a curtain of cold spray which wet my hair and beat a tattoo on my oilskin front before running down on to the top of the petrol tank over which I stood.

It seemed to take us a long while to reach the Dodman and I felt very tired. Sam looked as though he had had enough, but George, throwing an occasional glance over his shoulder to see how we were progressing, seemed none the worse, in spite of the fact that he had been working hardest of all. He was baiting up with the same easy speed, chewing his tobacco and spitting at regular intervals. He had little patience when things went wrong, but beneath his gruff exterior I felt he had a kind heart, and, provided we were home by opening time, he was prepared to tolerate our lack of knowledge and ability.

By a quarter to six we had entered the outer harbour and brought the *Coral* alongside the Lighthouse quay, where J.B.'s lorry was standing all ready for us to off-load our fish. Baskets were slung down, the net-room hatches were removed and George began to pile the dogfish into the baskets, while Sam and I lifted them out, attached the hooks to each handle and signalled Tony to hoist away on the little motor crane. When all the dogfish had gone we sent up the baskets of rays and turbots and the conger in a basket on its own. The conger, still alive, had got a great dogfish half down its throat. George dealt with this by jumping on the conger's stomach, which made the fish promptly divulge itself of the half-swallowed "dog." Finally, there remained

87

the skate. These were sent up singly, the hooks on the crane's ropes being inserted into the skates' mouths.

"Go on," said George. "Go and see them weighed in. We'll put her to her moorings." I climbed up the steps, still in thigh-boots and smock.

"Got a few dogs, then?" said Tony, who drove J.B.'s lorry. He was always friendly and helpful. "Hop on the back."

We drove along the outer harbour quay and into Edwards's store. There Waller and Tony whipped the baskets off the lorry and weighed the dogfish first. Then he weighed the basket of ray and conger and, finally, he put the great skates flat on the weighing machine.

"Bit of huffy here," said Waller, holding up the turbot.

"I thought there were two of them," I said.

"Only one here," said Tony.

"Oh well, I expect I'm muddling them up with a ray. In any case, what is huffy?"

"Well, it's like this, old man," said Waller. "If you get a lobster or a turbot or a crayfish or two, they fetch a lot of money, so instead of the usual sharing system, the money is split evenly between the crew."

Waller handed me my chit. I glanced at it. We'd caught 100 stone of fish. I wished them good night and went out to join Sam and George, who had already moored the *Coral.* I filled up the tanks and took along the two five-gallon drums to fill them with petrol and paraffin. I found those ten gallons heavy to carry, and when I returned, George was on the quayside.

"What time tomorrow, George?" I asked.

"Be down at five. Have you ordered another six stone of bait and some salt?"

"No," I admitted.

"Well, you'd better," he grunted. Then, turning, he handed me the other turbot.

"Here," he said, "send it home to your father and mother. It's your first turbot," and he was gone.

Holding the fish, I watched him go up a narrow alley-way, his massive figure rolling away in his white sea-boots, both hands thrust deep into his pockets, his red tin of food held under his arm, a splash of colour against his pale blue, much-washed smock. He turned once to spit and then was gone.

I ordered the salt and bait, showed Waller and Tony the missing turbot and, putting the ten gallons of fuel aboard the *Babs*, sculled her slowly out to the *Coral*. The tubs had all been covered, the legs shipped, the engine hatch closed. It was half-past six and we had finished our first day of lining. We secured the *Babs* and walked slowly home. I glanced at Sam and saw how tired he looked.

"See you at five," I said as we parted.

Once home, I gave the turbot to Biddie, took off my sea-boots and sank down into an armchair. Only then did I realise how weary I was. I drank hot tea and thought with horror of five o'clock next morning, when we would again start up our engines and repeat the whole performance. Gradually my tiredness wore off and I sat relaxed and content in mind, listening to the wireless, waiting for the weather forecast and watching the fire flickering in the grate.

CHAPTER SIX

Dogging and Spiltering

HARDLY had my head touched the pillow before I sank into a deep velvet oblivion, only to be dragged back to consciousness by the metallic clamour of our alarm clock. Whenever I am woken in this manner, for a brief moment, until I have vacated my bed, my heart sinks, my spirit is at its lowest and the prospect of facing the cold darkness of early morning fills me with something akin to fear. Although I was summoned scores of times during the war to go on the middle or morning watch, by the shrill whistle of the bosun's pipe, or a rough shake from a member of the opposite watch, I have never grown accustomed to this abrupt form of awakening.

There was a fine drizzle and sea mist about as I quietly closed the small iron gate behind me, waved goodbye to Biddie and headed across the field. Already I could hear the sound of the fishing boats' engines, and when the harbour came in view I could see through the wet, misty, early-morning air the vague shapes of a lugger or two moving gently forward, nosing their way towards the harbour entrance, above which the lighthouse sent out its yellow beam.

I was first down, so got the basket of bait and salt and put them both aboard the *Babs*. By the time I had done this George and Sam had arrived and we all went out to the *Coral*. We towed the *Babs* out with us and anchored her in the outer harbour, for it would be low water during the afternoon and the inner harbour would be dry.

Again we headed south, and Sam and I cut up the bait

while George steered, chewing his tobacco and at intervals turning his head to spit over the side. We shot our line once more off the Manacles, but this time further out to sea.

"Edgar Husband in the *Margaret* caught fifty stone yesterday," remarked George. This was news indeed, for he carried twice as many hooks as we did; yet, in spite of this, we had caught twice as many fish. I was thinking how well we'd done when I was smartly brought down to earth by George's next remark.

"You can have a go at pulling the line today," he said as he opened his tin of food and took out a great sandwich.

I thought, or certainly hoped, that I had detected a suspicion of a smile in his glance. Ah well, I thought to myself, I've got to learn, and the sooner I get on with it the better.

The weather was fine and the sea flat as George brought

the *Coral* gently alongside the dan buoy. Leaning over, I lifted it aboard and began to haul and coil the eighty fathoms of dan line. In no time the line was up and down, and with my knee against the side of the boat, I leant back on the line till I felt the tension of the rope suddenly lessen and I knew that I had broken the anchor out of the bottom.

"Creeper's aweigh," I called.

"Well, haul it up, man. Haul the damn thing up," answered George.

Before the creeper was out of the water I could see the line attached to one of its flukes slanting downwards into the water with those green shapes on either side. As soon as I had the creeper aboard, I passed it to George, who took off the line from the creeper's fluke.

"Pull the line steadily," called George as the first dogfish came dangling over the side, twisting and turning. I grabbed for it with my right hand, very conscious of that wicked spur. I missed the twisting body and grabbed again.

"Get hold of it, man," roared George.

At the third attempt, more frightened of George than the fish, I caught the creature by the back of the head with my right hand and felt its cold, coarse skin. With my left hand I grasped the shank of the hook between the thumb and the index finger, at the same time still holding the line with this hand. Then, twisting both hands quickly, there was a slight grating sound as though a tooth were being drawn and the hook came free from the fish's mouth. Finally, with a movement of my wrist, I sent the creature spinning through the dark hole of the net-room, where a single plank had been removed, and heard it land on the *Coral's* bottom boards with a dull thud.

I had handled my first dogfish and here came the second, and down below in the dark water I could see a good many more. Gradually I became more certain in the handling of the fish and was able to glance at George as he stood tending the wheel and engine and baiting up. Sam stood alongside me, tall, with his head bent slightly over his tub as he slowly and methodically baited his hooks. Suddenly I felt the line tighten.

"Is she fast?" called George.

"Seems like it," I replied.

He brought the boat gently ahead and into the line, which was quivering with tautness and beginning to slip through my hands. I held on grimly, for there was a tub half full of line on my right side containing some 150 hooks. I did not at all like the idea of the line taking charge and the hooks flying through my hands. During the war a Belgian fisherman, fishing from Mevagissey, had been hooked and taken over on the line. They had pulled him in almost at once, but he was dead. Something now had to give. I could see George watching the line and my face closely.

"Catch hold of the line," he shouted to Sam, but before the latter could move I felt the line give way, and the hauling went on as before. George gave me a meaning look.

"What do you do, George, when that happens?" I asked.

"Hang on," he answered laconically.

There were not so many fish on the line as yesterday, but it looked as though there were enough to make the trip financially worthwhile. All at once the line felt heavy.

"Feels as though there's something weighty down there, George," I remarked.

"Skate," he answered.

He was right. Far down below I caught sight of a great greenish shape. Then suddenly the line came away easily. I thought he'd gone, but he was only swimming up with the line. Now he was in full sight, a magnificent fish. He lay broadside on and I pulled hard at the line. To my dismay, I saw him break free.

"Pull steadily," shouted George, angrily.

Astonished, I saw the great fish swim up and take another bait. Again he went broadside on to the line some 10 feet under the surface. Again I pulled the line too hard and lost him.

"Don't jerk the line so," called George in exasperation.

Once more the great bat-like creature took another hook. It suddenly occurred to me as I watched this that the fish could neither be afraid nor hurt. This time I did not lose the skate and, leaning over, we both gaffed him and dragged him up over the side and on to the net-room hatches, where he lay hissing and gasping.

By now the line had cut into my hands, my arms and back were aching and I was working more slowly. I had pulled nearly five tubs of line and there were still some 1,300 hooks to pull. Suddenly George knocked the engine out of gear and climbed over the net-room hatches. Without a word he took over the line and I took up his position in the stern.

Shortly after one o'clock the line was all in and we were homeward bound. We made good headway, and shortly after four in the afternoon we were alongside the outer harbour steps, unloading our fish. Before I went in to watch the fish weighed, I filled up the *Coral's* tanks. Then I climbed up the steps, and jumped on to the back of Tony's lorry, and with the two empty fuel drums alongside me, we motored round the outer harbour and into J.B.'s store. There the fish were weighed once again and I saw from the chit that we had caught 57 stone.

I ordered another six stone of bait and then picked up the two empty five-gallon drums.

"Buck up and fill 'em," called Tony. "I'll be going out again directly. If you're quick you can hop aboard the lorry."

I hurried back with the fuel and was just in time to put the two drums on to the back of the lorry and jump on again. In no time we were back at the steps, down which I carried the fuel. I very much disliked carrying these ten gallons of fuel at the end of a day's fishing, for not only were the drums heavy to carry, but awkward to grip.

We took the *Coral* into the middle of the outer harbour, where we anchored her fore and aft. It was necessary to leave her here for the night, as there would be no water in the inner harbour at five the following morning. We finished

baiting up our lines and all three climbed into the *Babs*.
There was just enough water for us to moor the pram round
the southern corner of the inner harbour.

For the rest of the week we met at five each morning,
motored off for some three or four hours, shot and hauled
our line, motored back baiting up hard all the while, and
finished usually between five and six in the evening. They
were full days, and I would return every evening, tired and
satiated with sea air, to a quiet welcome from Biddie. In
these early days I must have been a dull companion in the
evenings, for I was physically incapable of anything but
sitting quietly before the fire, feeling the efforts of the day's
work seeping out of my very bones. Biddie was a tower of
strength to me, for she showed great sympathy and never
demanded my attention.

J.B. paid me on Saturday and in the loft I shared out our
money with Sam and George. We had not done too badly,
for we had caught 297 stone of fish, and when the expenses
of fuel and bait had been deducted there was some £28 to
share. Sam received £7 and George and I £10 10s. 0d.
apiece, for George and I split the boat's share. I was
never to earn as much again when lining, although we
worked just as hard.

On Saturday afternoon we moved down to Mary Husband, taking sufficient clothes to last us ten days. Mrs
Church had kindly said she would keep the remainder of our
possessions until we moved into our flat.

Mary Husband lived just above the harbour on the
north side, less than a minute's walk from the quayside. No
cars could reach this little alley, with its whitewashed stone
cottages, thick, irregular walls and small windows, a sure
protection against the wild winter nights, when the wind
would thunder in from the sea and seek out every sheltered
nook and cranny. Some of these cottages are joined by
passages, a relic of the days of smuggling when contraband
could be off-loaded and run up through the cottages to the
top of the cliffs and then away inland. Mary Husband's

cottage had an archway leading into a yard which in the old days would have contained nets and lines and salted fish for the winter months. Her front door lay just inside this archway, on the right-hand side. We knocked, and Mary Husband herself opened the door and asked us to come in.

We found ourselves at once in the main eating- and living-room. There was a fair-sized rectangular table around which were placed six chairs. Two easy chairs stood on either side of the fireplace. In one of these crouched an old man, poking the fire. A settee lay up against the window, an upright piano stood against another wall and a sideboard ran along the fourth wall.

"I'll show you your room," said Mary Husband. She breathed heavily as we followed her up a narrow flight of stairs.

"I've put you in here," she panted. "I'll just go and put a kettle on for tea."

The room was small and the two beds did not look very comfortable. I had noticed a peculiar smell down below and I could smell it in our bedroom too. I suddenly felt depressed and shut in. With difficulty I opened the window. Biddie, however, was in great form, completely unmoved by it all and quite certain that Mary Husband was a dear. How right she was.

"After all," she pointed out, "Mary has taken us in and we ought to be grateful. She's also charging us very little."

"You're quite right," I said. "We'll go down and have a cup of tea and a walk round the village before the shops close."

We bought a few things we needed for the week-end. I noticed how friendly everyone was towards Biddie. They had accepted her and were ready to help her as the fishermen had helped me. We walked out along the quay, and there was always a nod and a friendly word called out to us whenever we passed the fishermen. We walked back and came upon Peter Barron, dressed in his best clothes.

"I hear you're staying with Mary Husband," he began. "The missus and I would like you both to come and have tea with us tomorrow." We thanked him warmly and said we would be delighted to come.

Back in Mary Husband's living-room a late high tea was being prepared. The old man still crouched over the grate, but there were now two others in the room, a man and a child. Mr Close had a facial paralysis, which made his speech very difficult to understand. He had slipped and fallen on his back when climbing up a wooden pile at low water in Looe Harbour. He owned the *Manxman*, a small lugger which fished for him. He had been at Oxford and would talk to me of pre-war Oxford times. I liked him and he had a lot of courage.

The child was a girl of ten. I believe she had been evacuated during the war and now seemed to live permanently with Mary Husband. She had one terrifying habit which she practised all through the day, particularly during meals. She chewed bubble-gum, with which she would make a very sharp little explosion. I could tolerate it during the day provided I did not inadvertently put my hand on a piece of chewing-gum which she had left lying around. But to see her suddenly in the middle of a meal put a piece into her mouth, a piece which had been resting conveniently on the dining table, and contort her mouth in such a way as to produce this sharp explosion, made me feel positively ill.

Mary did not notice it; I suppose by now she had grown accustomed to the explosions. Nor did the old man worry, but then he was deaf and heard very little except when Mary called him to stop poking the fire, which invariably sent him into a paroxysm of rage and reduced Mary to deep silent gusts of laughter. Mr Close, however, liked it as little as I did, but he was too fond of Mary to say anything. I could see she was a great help to him, for under her easy-going roof he could live a normal life, close to the two things he loved most, the sea and his boat.

Those ten days we spent with Mary Husband were truly

extraordinary. I quickly found out that the cats were responsible for that peculiar smell which sifted all through the house. There were three or four enormous cats which would leap up on to the kitchen table with a silent and effortless grace, and once there crouch defiantly amongst the innumerable pots and pans, dishes and cups, all waiting to be washed up. I have only to close my eyes to see Mary sitting upright with one of these great cats in her lap, on the left side of the fireplace. Biddie and I would sit on the sofa. Suddenly and to my horror, for I am no cat-lover and so had been keeping a wary eye open, a huge cat would unexpectedly leap upon my knees, and as I moved in involuntary revulsion sharp claws would dig into me. Almost at once there would be a loud crack from the bubble-gum, followed by Mary's tenth request : "Go to bed, Peggy."

Mary Husband was a very large woman who moved slowly, resigned to the fact that her wind was short and her feet painful. She had fair hair and a friendly, round face, smooth and unworried. She was placid and benign, the cares of the world had put no mark upon her, for she had refused to bow to them. Her movements were slow and deliberate but her mind was shrewd and active. As she sat of an evening in her straight-backed chair, looking into the fire, with one of her enormous cats lying motionless on her lap, its head up and eyes closed, I wondered at first whether she bothered to listen to the general conversation around her. I very soon found out that she heard everything and was surprisingly well-informed on many matters. When we discussed topical problems she always had something to say, not only interesting but which showed an appreciative assessment of both sides of a problem ; she had a good sense of humour, if at times a naughty one.

Her brother Joe would often come up for an hour in the evening. He was a huge man and always wore a blue suit and an old yachting cap. He would be given a cup of tea by Mary and then he would sit straight upright, very like his sister, saying little but smiling all the time.

We continued dogging hard for the next fortnight, catching between 40 and 50 stone a day. The days were fine and the sea calm, for summer and the month of June were at hand. Several times recently I had heard the word "spiltering" used, and twice during his evening visits Willie had asked when we were going to put our spilter line aboard.

One Friday afternoon as I steered the *Coral* through the outer harbour after a long day of dogging—all that week we had been leaving at half-past four in the morning—George abruptly announced that we would start spiltering the following week. I walked home that late May afternoon happy and content, for we had completed a full week of fishing and prospects of a restful week-end lay ahead.

I awoke at a civilised hour next morning and went down to a hot, unhurried breakfast, sitting at a table instead of leaning against the side of a pitching boat some fifteen miles offshore. By nine I was down on the quay.

"Got your pay yet?" called Edgar. "George and Sam are up in the loft waiting. They've been there these past two hours and George is getting impatient; it won't be long before it's opening time!"

I laughed. "Just going," I called back.

J.B.'s daughter paid me our week's earnings and I went into our loft, where Sam and George had just arrived. There we shared out our money. When this was done, George stayed behind in the loft working on the spilter line, while Sam and I went down and brought our nine tubs of long line ashore in the *Babs*. These we carried upstairs to the loft. We then took off all the hooks and put them in a large tin. Finally, we hung the lines out of our loft to dry, before taking them over to Joe Furse, where we would bark and tar them in preparation for another season.

The spilter line was worked in exactly the same way as the dog line, but was thinner and had smaller hooks, although we still worked the same number.

The shank of the hook was little more than an inch long

with a flat piece at the end, whereas the dog hook had an eye at the end through which was passed the strop. With the spilter hook we had to bend the tarred strop on to the shank of the hook with a clove hitch. This took time, and as the line and the strops were full of tar, it was messy work as well. At one o'clock we finished for the week-end and it was clear we would have a busy day on Monday, finishing

making up the spilter line in the morning and baiting it up in the afternoon. But for the moment work was finished, the week-end lay ahead and the weather looked settled.

At the week-ends Biddie and I would go for long walks over the cliffs, or if it was warm enough, we might wander down to a beach where she could bathe and I would lie on the sand and watch the clouds in the sky. We would talk about our first eventful months in Mevagissey and discuss the future, and not once did either of us feel the slightest regret for that chance encounter with George Allen. For that meeting alone we had much to thank George Allen for.

We went to tea with Peter Barron and his wife on Sunday afternoon. Their tiny parlour was immaculately clean and they could not have been more welcoming. They plied us with good home-made jam and cream, all laid out on a snow white tablecloth. After tea Mrs Barron chattered away to Biddie while Peter showed me photographs of his son and talked about fishing and how it had been good during the war, but very bad at times between the two wars.

"We're putting our spilter line aboard tomorrow," I told him.

"'Ess," he said. "So are we. You'll find it a fiddly old job to begin with."

"Is it very different from dogging?" I asked.

"No," he said, "but it's longish hours and you'll find it

tedious work until you get the hang of it. George is a good man and he'll show you what it's all about."

We said good night to Peter and his wife and thanked them both warmly.

"You must come again, my dears," she said as we went down the steps of her front door and into the crooked and narrow little alleyway that led to Mary Husband's cottage.

We had already had a week with Mary and the following Saturday had planned to move into our summer flat. In spite of the cats and the sharp bubble-gum explosions, the peculiar smell and the incredible muddle in the kitchen, I had grown very attached to this household with its strange and varied occupants. Time did not seem to matter; speed of movement was inessential and unlikely. Meals were never hurried affairs which began and finished at certain hours, but leisurely occasions when many cups of tea were drunk and Mary, at regular intervals, would pad slowly from the direction of the kitchen, carrying a freshly made pot of tea and breathing heavily.

All Monday morning we worked hard to finish making up the spilter line, only breaking off to visit Uncle Dick. In the afternoon we collected a basket of bait from J.B.'s store. Our bait for the spilter line was mackerel. It was more expensive than pilchard bait and the cutting-up required more skill. Holding the mackerel by its head and putting it flat on the bait board, we would insert the knife just below the gills and with one clean sweep down the backbone, cut a fillet from that side of the mackerel. Turning the fish over we would do the same to the other side, leaving two fillets of mackerel. These would then be cut straight down the middle, making four strips of mackerel which in turn would be cut into six to eight small pieces. So from one mackerel there would be 24 to 30 baits.

I enjoyed cutting up mackerel, for the fish were much firmer, and I found that after a short time I could, once the initial cut had been made, fillet them without looking at them; the feel of the blade down the backbone was the guide. The hooks were baited in the same way as a dog hook, but, of course, it was more fiddly work, somewhat relieved by the fact that the baits were firmer.

Willie came along and gave us a hand during the afternoon, and by five o'clock we had finished the baiting-up and put the tubs aboard the *Coral*. I fuelled the *Coral*, cleaned the plugs and the jets and went ashore. We arranged to meet down at the quay at three-thirty the following morning.

I was in bed by nine that night and was woken at three by the alarm. I dressed quickly, made myself a cup of tea and ate a slice of bread and butter. I filled my thermos flask with hot tea, picked up my tin of sandwiches and stepped out of Mary's front door into total darkness.

I felt the wind on my face, heard it sigh and fall, only to regain strength quickly as it buffeted the thick, uneven chimney breasts and the heavy stone-slated roofs of the huddled cottages. I knew if we went out today we should have a rough old time of it, for I already had enough knowledge to know at once what it would be like at sea from the direction and strength of the wind inshore.

I found at once that no boats had gone out, though the crews were all down on the quayside. I joined Sam and George and watched the various groups, dark figures standing in the yellow light thrown by the odd few lamps scattered around the harbour. Some of them walked out along the north sea wall and stood looking out to sea. They were waiting, undecided whether to go to sea or not.

All at once their indecision was shaken by the noise of an engine starting up, followed by the slow, deliberate beat of a diesel. In a moment all eyes were on the dark shape of a lugger that was already going astern before pushing slowly ahead into the outer harbour and away. It was the signal for action, and with one accord the crews went out to their boats, started up their engines and got under way.

Before we had got outside the Gwineas we had all donned our oilskins. Under the fishing light we cut up our bait. We spoke no words, for that hour before dawn is not much of a time for conversation. I wondered what George and Sam were thinking about as they stood cutting up their bait facing aft. George had handed over the wheel to me and given me a south-easterly course to steer. Within an hour we had finished cutting up the bait and could relax for the next two hours until we reached the fishing ground. All around boats were heading in the same direction as ourselves.

Dawn was a grey affair with low clouds and plenty of wind. I had to watch out that I didn't give Sam and George a wetting, for the seas were running on to our starboard bow and the wind was strong and would whip the spray clean across the boat.

I looked around and recognised a number of the boats accompanying us. There were several toshers—one-man boats who motored the eighteen miles offshore and shot and hauled their lines entirely on their own.

Three and a half hours after we had left Mevagissey Light we shut down the Kelvin. We had reached the fishing grounds, a sandy patch on the bottom of the sea some five miles square, where the whiting come for a short spell during the summer months of June, July and August.

Most of the boats had begun shooting their lines, all in the same direction and more or less in a long row. George manœuvred the *Coral* into a good position, a fair distance from the next boat. This was very important, for if the tide was strong and we were too close to the next boat, our line might carry down and across with the current till it fouled our neighbour's line, a quite appalling thought.

It was seven o'clock as we began motoring slowly back to the western dan buoy, eating our breakfast on the way. I steered the *Coral* up to the buoy, which was bobbing and ducking wildly in the short, sharp seas. The procedure for pulling a spilter line is no different from that required for hauling a dog line. In came the eighty fathoms of dan line, up came the creeper with the spilter line attached, and the long pull had begun.

At first the fish were scarce, but gradually they began to come, mostly whiting, with here and there an odd ray or turbot, ling or monkfish. The last-named was an extraordinary fish with a short body and a huge mouth, capable of containing a small football. It always astonished me that they paid us 5s. 6d. a pound for this fish. George pulled steadily, periodically calling on me to go ahead when the line was fast on the bottom. He had great strength and would hold the quivering line tight while he waited for it to jerk free. He seemed to concentrate harder when this happened, and even stopped chewing. Suddenly the line would go free and he would immediately spit over the side and give me a stern look, as though I had been down on the bottom of the line holding it fast. So we progressed, George hauling, Sam steadily baiting-up, whilst I kept the *Coral* heading gently into the line, baiting-up when I could and periodically glancing over the side at the slanting line of fish.

"Gaff," George suddenly shouted.

Looking over the side, I saw a turbot coming up on the line, with another swimming behind, apparently unattached.

"Gaff the second turbot first," said George.

I put the gaff quietly into the water and with a quick jerk gaffed this second turbot. Having dropped him into the net-room, I leant over and gaffed the first turbot, which was on the hook.

"Never haul a turbot out of the water," said George. "He'll always drop off."

"Funny thing that other fish swimming up," I remarked.

"Often happens that the turbot will swim up after its mate that's hooked," he replied.

After another hour George called me to pull the line. I found it much thinner, and at once I could feel it cutting into the index finger of my right hand. I changed my grip; and my little finger began to take punishment. Later that day George showed me how to make finger stalls from an old rubber inner tube. The line seemed to have gone over a field of starfish, and for a short distance there was one on every hook. These I quickly removed and flung back into the sea. Every so often a gurnet would come up on the line, a nasty little red fish, full of sharp spurs. One did not touch these fish, but with a quick flick shook them free of the hook. Some of the fish, such as cod and ling, floated up on the line when they neared the surface. Looking down, I saw a fine 3-lb. lobster coming up.

"Don't pull him out or he'll drop off," and, leaning over with a basket, George scooped up the lobster. We caught the occasional sole and a few dogfish, which now felt excessively hard and rough after the soft, silky feel of the whiting.

At last, after two hours' pulling, the dan buoy was alongside, and, leaning over, I lifted it aboard. It had been hard work and I looked at my fingers, where the line had made raw places. I clambered aft and started up the Kelvin. We all had a bite of food and a hot drink from our flasks. Then we began to bait up the line again for the following day. The seas were now on our port quarter, lifting us up and thrusting us homewards. It was gone noon as we headed for the coast, which was barely visible. There was no break in the low clouds overhead; to the north a slanting grey curtain of rain joined sea and sky. The weather looked bad and I was glad we were homeward bound.

I soon appreciated what Peter Barron meant when he said spiltering was tedious. As I turned the line out of the tub and on to the deckboards and saw that great heap of uncleared line, with its mass of little hooks with their strops wrapped round the main line, it appeared to me an appalling muddle and a horrifying task. The thought that this had to be cleared and baited before three o'clock next morning was a grim one.

It was far slower work than clearing and baiting up a dog line. For one thing, a spilter hook is not so easy to get hold of as a dog hook. Again, one seems to lose many more hooks in spiltering, and these all have to be replaced.

Finally, there is the strop's maddening habit of wrapping itself round the main line. George saw me slowly and laboriously trying to unwind a strop and showed me a very simple and quick method. This involved hanging the hook on the main line, then holding the latter in front of one's chest and spinning the line in the opposite direction. In this way the strop would be unravelled from the main line.

As I now stood baiting up these interminable hooks, it didn't take me long to work out that if I baited up 900 hooks and took ten seconds over each one, two and a half hours would have passed before I finished the job. This would not be at all bad, but it also became equally as clear to me a little later that by the time I had replaced hooks, cleared the line, baited it up and coiled it down in the tub, my average would be nearer fifteen seconds and probably more, taking me not far short of four hours to bait my part of the line. We usually arrived back in the harbour between half-past three or four in the afternoon. Once inside the harbour, there were the fish to be taken ashore and weighed, the engines to be attended to, fuel to be fetched and on top of all this, a good hour's baiting-up to be done, before the line was completed. I would be lucky if I was on my way home by half-past five. The secret, of course, is to waste not a second of time, but seize the line and work at it without a stop, not pausing to talk or look up, making sure that the replacement of hooks and other repairs do not take much longer than the actual baiting of a hook.

It always fascinated me watching the silent speed and concentration of a crew when they were baiting-up. They were all racing the clock; the sooner it was finished the sooner they would be ashore.

It was gone half-past five before Sam and I had finished this our first day of spiltering. We each took a few whiting home for supper.

I opened Mary Husband's front door, took off my seaboots and went into the sitting-room. There I found Biddie writing a letter at the table. Over in the corner the old man was still sitting crouched over the fire. I held up the whiting in front of her.

"Hello. Like a cup of tea?" she asked, taking the fish from me. I smiled and nodded and she disappeared into the kitchen.

The wireless was on and the weather forecast was just beginning. I leant against the upright piano and listened. I noticed the old man in the corner was trying to catch the forecast as well, for he too had been a fisherman. Everyone listens to the weather forecast in a fishing village, for on it so much can depend. The clear, concise voice of the announcer filled the room: "Viking, Cromarty, Forth, Tyne, Dogger . . ." I waited, and then it was our turn— "Wight, Portland, Plymouth. Strong south-easterly winds increasing to gale force. . . ."

I had heard enough.

I drank the hot tea which Biddie had brought in and went upstairs to wash and shave. My hands smarted when I put them in the warm water.

After supper we strolled down to the harbour. Everyone knew the forecast and it was generally considered that no boats would go out tomorrow. I saw George and Sam and we went up to them.

"Have a look at it at six," said George. "If it's blowing hard there's no point in coming down."

We all looked up at the low clouds as they raced across the leaden sky.

"The cone's up," said Sam, indicating the coastguard station with a jerk of his head.

On the way home we stopped and, leaning over the wall, looked down at the harbour. All boats were at their moorings. A few visitors were wandering disconsolately around the quayside. Even the gulls seemed subdued. A drop of rain fell heavily as we turned and made our way back to Mary Husband's cottage.

CHAPTER SEVEN

The Coming of Kim

WE moved that week-end into the bungalow which we had rented up to the second week of September. This was our first taste of living entirely on our own. Here we had no landlady to watch over us, nor did we have to share our sitting-room. This was ours and we basked in our privacy. Apart from a fair-sized sitting-room, three bedrooms and a kitchen, we had the sheer luxury of a bathroom with an immersion heater.

Sunday night was dark and cold and we both wondered what the weather would be like at three o'clock the following morning. Some of the boats were going out even earlier and it appeared to be developing into a race to reach the fishing grounds first.

I awoke before the alarm and, leaning over, pressed the button to stop it from ringing. I lay quietly for a moment, listening to the wind stirring the rambler rose that framed part of our bedroom window. The weather didn't sound too good. I made a quick cup of tea and gave one to Biddie, who was by now awake. It was time to go; in my sea-boots and smock, with a scarf round my neck and my tin of food under my arm, I felt very much the primeval hunter going forth, as I leant over the bed and kissed Biddie's warm cheek.

Sam and George were waiting and, without any ado, we all three went out to the *Coral* and I started the engines. For three hours little was said. The morning was sullen and angry as we began to shoot the line. The forecast had said the weather would improve later in the morning, and as we motored slowly back to the western dan it looked as though it was already brightening. Over to starboard Nipper Lee and his crew had started getting in their line. It struck me that we were closer than usual to the next boat. I noticed that the tide was ebbing strongly, for the line floated down and away from the *Coral*. The sun suddenly broke through the cloud and the sea sparkled, and, looking down into the water, I could see we had caught a good few whiting.

We always kept some baskets aboard, and into these George threw the whiting. We had two baskets full, about twelve stone, when I happened to glance across at Nipper Lee. I was astonished and not a little alarmed to see how close we now were to his boat. I looked quickly at George and it was clear that he too was concerned by the nearness of the two boats. I went on baiting my line and tending the wheel and engine, but every so often I glanced out of the corner of my eye to see if we were any nearer Nipper Lee's boat. Nipper's crew too were now turning frequently in their work and glancing across at us as the distance between the two boats lessened. There was no doubt about it: we were drawing closer and closer every moment. All the time no word was said, which to me made the tension far worse. I looked at Sam and I could see he was obviously as worried as I was.

Suddenly I heard Nipper Lee shout and saw him point in our direction. The boats were by now very close. One of his crew went forward and passed the line around their bow in order to pull it in on the port side. With a sinking feeling I looked down at our line and there, to my horror, saw what we had all secretly suspected: our line had fouled Nipper Lee's. It looked quite frightful, and to make matters worse there were plenty of fish on both the lines.

"Bloody hell, George," I heard Nipper shout in anger.

George acknowledged with a grunt and a bit of a smile, followed by a long stream of tobacco juice. He did not seem particularly perturbed, but I could see that Nipper and his crew were far from pleased. It was, of course, our fault for we had shot our line up-tide of Nipper and too close. The result was that the strong current had carried our line down and across his.

It fell to George Pearce to do the clearing, which he did most skilfully. I have never in my life seen so many hooks and such a tangle. While Nipper Lee held on to his line, George pulled our line, with theirs attached. He cleared the taut and quivering strops by somehow disentangling the hooks and taking off the fish. Nipper, working now on his port side, pulled his line bit by bit as George disentangled the two lines. It was tricky work, and several times I thought George would be caught by one of the flying hooks; the tension on the lines would whip a hook through the air at lightning speed. I had a bait-knife at hand and many times had to cut a strop which refused to be cleared. A lot of the fish were falling off the hooks and those in my reach I gaffed before they floated away. Nipper's crew did the same.

After an hour and a half of this tense work the lines suddenly parted and we were each able to haul them separately. I tried tactfully to find out what George thought about it all, but apart from a remark to the effect that Nipper seemed to be a bit annoyed, I could get very little out of him.

By now the sun was out and although the wind was still strong, the weather was brighter and looked more settled. George finished pulling the lines and we returned home.

Once inside I suggested that we should give Nipper Lee a basket and a half of whiting, as I had noticed that he seemed to have more fish on his line and that some of the whiting I had gaffed were obviously his. Apart from anything else it would be a gesture.

"Please yourself," said George dryly, but not unkindly. I looked at Sam.

"I should give them to him," he said. "It'll do no harm."

I carried them over to Nipper and his crew.

"Here you are," I said. "So sorry we fouled your line."

"George bloody well should have known better," remarked Abe May, and John Gill nodded in agreement.

"That's all right mate," said Nipper as he took the baskets. "These things do happen, and it might have been worse."

I stood on the quayside looking down at them as they baited their hooks with extraordinary speed. I felt awkward, for I didn't quite know what to say.

"Yes," I said after a moment or two of silence, and turned to go. Suddenly I heard Nipper call after me.

"You got a few yourselves, didn't you?" And as I turned I could see by their faces that they were now all rather amused over the whole affair and had quite forgiven us.

I returned to the *Coral* and began to bait up my line.

"All right?" said Sam.

"Yes," I replied. "They seemed rather pleased."

"So they bloody well should be," said George with a laugh and an extra juicy spit for good measure.

On the way home that evening I ran into Edgar Husband, who had long ago finished and was now on his way down to the quay.

"What be you a-doing today?" he said and then he began to laugh silently. "Did George shoot over Nipper Lee's line?" he managed to ask at last.

"He did indeed," I replied, "and I hope I never see such a sight again. Into the bargain, George wants us down at two-thirty tomorrow morning."

At this Edgar bent forward, put both hands on his knees and rocked with silent laughter. I couldn't help laughing myself.

All at once he straightened up, his face now serious, though tears ran down his cheeks.

"Never mind, old man. You'm get along home and have your tea."

"I think I'd better," I said. "It's six o'clock now and that damned alarm will be going off in a few hours' time."

"Yes," he said; "it will," and this seemed to make him laugh harder than ever.

I never tired of Edgar's company and he never changed.

All that week we fished hard, leaving harbour at half-past two in the morning and sometimes, if the weather was bad, later. But it was during those early hours of the morning when the weather was bad and no one was prepared to make a start, that I used to feel really depressed. My thoughts turned towards the warm bed I had left and the long hours of tedious work ahead. Yet here we were all just waiting and watching the sky. It meant that our day was going to be so much longer. The fishermen would walk up and down, talking quietly. Others would lean against the wall under J.B.'s office, waiting patiently, quite resigned to the fact that the weather was against them. I wondered why they didn't sit down and rest their legs, for they would be standing for the next fourteen or fifteen hours. I used to sit down and, leaning back against the wall with arms folded, close my eyes. I never slept but I felt that at least I was saving my energy for the hours of work that lay ahead of us.

We continued spiltering through June and, apart from one fine week, the weather was foul and the catches small. There was difficulty at times in getting enough bait for the boats, for there was a scarcity of mackerel. I enjoyed that one week of fine weather, for there is nothing nicer than being on the water when the sun is hot and the sea calm. I took Biddie out twice during this week and she thoroughly enjoyed herself. I wondered how George would react when Biddie was aboard. He couldn't have been nicer, and took a delight in handing her scallops to eat. We used to get a good number clinging to the line. George would prize them open with his bait-knife and, cleaning away the uneatable part, would hand her the scallop shell with the white edible piece in the centre. It was good food and she ate with enjoyment.

Our line was attacked several times by sharks. One could not only feel them, but see them as they swam around down below, taking our whiting. To deal with these sharks we had a long pole in the boat at the end of which was lashed a sharp metal spike. Sometimes the sharks would come right up with the line and then George would call on me to go to work with our home-made spear. Leaning over, I would stab at them and they would disappear with a swirl to deeper water, where they would continue to attack the line. They were a very real menace, for not only would they take the fish off the hooks, but sometimes even bite through the line. When this happened it meant going to the eastern dan buoy, pulling up the creeper and starting to haul from that end. If the sharks still continued attacking the fish, the line might be bitten through a second time. This meant that a length of line lay on the bottom of the sea. The only method of regaining it was to drag a creeper backwards and forwards across what we judged to be the middle of the line.

Boats would creep for hour after hour and sometimes they never retrieved their line. But more often than not their patience was rewarded and the line was hauled up. It could mean a financial loss to them, even if they did retrieve the line, for if it was in a bad state the crew might be kept in for a day making good the damage. And it could happen that this was a day when all boats had fine catches.

Too soon, those five days of hot summer were over. The wind went round to the south-east again and we knew no more the calm sea and blue sky of that one June week.

We spent most of that week-end on the beach, and on Sunday evening our nearest neighbours, Jimmy and Beryl Earl, invited us in for a drink. They had a friend staying with them who was apparently most anxious to come out fishing with us; he was seriously considering buying a boat and fishing for his living.

"It struck me," said Jimmy, "that you'd be just the man to take Bill Hurrell out and show him the ropes."

"I'd be delighted to do so," I replied, "and he can come out when he likes and as often as he likes."

"What about tomorrow?" said Bill.

"Fine," I said. "We leave at half-past two. Do you think you can manage that frightful hour? At any rate I'll call for you at about two twenty and we can go down together."

There was plenty of wind the following morning and I

was in two minds whether to warn him that the weather did not look good. Eventually I decided to say nothing, for I thought it better that he should see the more realistic side of fishing before taking the plunge and buying a boat. He was already waiting outside Jimmy and Beryl's house and together we walked down to the quayside.

"This is Bill," I said to George and Sam, who had already arrived. Sam shook him warmly by the hand, but George couldn't even muster a grunt, though he did manage to spit and mutter, "Best get aboard."

It was blowing strongly from the south-east, and I handed over the wheel to Bill, giving him a course to steer.

"This is the life," he sang out, so obviously enjoying himself. George looked up sharply and gave Bill a long incredulous stare, and then spat before continuing his baiting-up.

Dawn came angry and red and ahead of us the sea looked grey and desolate, yet Bill was still in great form, laughing when spray went across the boat. After three and a half hours we reached the fishing grounds and I wondered whether he would be all right when we began to shoot the line.

"Go up forward, Bill, and you'll be in a better position to watch everything," I suggested to him.

I shut off the Kelvin and at once the *Coral* began to slither up, over, and down the growing seas. Before the first tub of line was shot Bill was leaning over, retching violently. I felt desperately sorry for him, but there was nothing we could do and he would have to stick it out for the next eight or nine hours. The weather deteriorated rapidly, and it was with relief that I saw the eastern dan buoy lurching wildly in the rough seas just off our starboard bow. I started up the Kelvin and called Sam to take over the wheel. Then I went forward to see Bill, who was stretched flat on his back in the bottom of the boat, with his eyes shut.

"How are you, Bill?" I asked him.

He stirred weakly and tried to smile, but I could see he had had more than enough. I squatted beside him. "Look,"

I said. "We're under way now and the motion won't be so upsetting. See if you can sit up on this thwart and get some fresh air."

I helped him into a sitting position and then went aft to take over the wheel and continue baiting-up. It was high tide when we got back and we tied up alongside the quayside opposite J.B.'s store. I gave Bill a hand up to the quay.

"Thanks," he said and gave George and Sam a wave as he stood, swaying unsteadily.

"Will you be all right?" I asked him.

"Yes, thanks," he replied. "I think I'll get along home," and with that he set off slowly and shakily along the quayside.

I jumped down into the boat and went on baiting-up.

"Is he coming out tomorrow?" asked George with a twinkle in his eye.

"Poor sod will think twice before he goes fishing again," Sam remarked.

Bill had picked a bad day for his initiation to fishing. But perhaps it was intended that he should go no further with his ambition. I couldn't help wondering whether I would have bought the *Coral* if I had undergone the same experience as Bill. I heard later that he had spent twenty-four hours in bed recovering.

One evening Jimmy Earl came over and asked me if I would like to play cricket for St Austell. I told him I would be delighted. That night I rang up my home and asked them to send down my cricket bag and all available flannels, shirts, socks and sweaters.

Three days later my gear arrived and that evening I unpacked it all before Willie's unbelieving eyes. He shook his head frequently and chuckled to himself.

"Does he know what to do with all that stuff, Missus?" he asked.

On Saturday I played for St Austell. I kept wicket and

made forty-odd runs. The ground was not very attractive, but I had some enjoyable games with the Club. We had a left-arm spinner called Griffiths who had a lot of ability and spun the ball viciously, particularly his Chinaman. Sometimes when keeping wicket to him I would go the wrong way behind the stumps and he would roar with laughter as the ball beat the bat, myself and first slip and went down for byes.

Later in the season I came across the Gorran Cricket Club, who rightly regarded themselves as champions of eastern Cornwall. They were immensely keen and their friendly, ruddy, wind-swept faces peered out from under their blue Australian-cut cricket caps. I remember well my first contact with the Gorran Cricket Club because we had lost several quick wickets to Archie Smith, their tall left-arm fast bowler.

Archie was a magnificent-looking person in his early twenties. He was every bit of six-foot-three, broad and very powerfully built. He would look one fair and square in the eyes with a face that was both strong and sunny.

I watched him now as he caught the ball with his left hand, turning at the same time to walk back to the beginning of his run-up. His hair was almost white, and to my astonishment was held in place by a hair-net. All the time I knew and played with Archie Smith, I never heard anyone mention this hair-net. He wore it on all occasions, even when he was playing for the county. He is still wearing it and is still a first and natural choice for Cornwall, and will be for many years to come. I watched him toss the ball up in the air and catch it again in his left hand and I noticed how completely the ball was engulfed in that huge fist. He gave me a friendly smile as he passed on his way to his bowling mark. I saw him turn smoothly, run up to the wicket and bowl a good-length ball outside the off stump which moved in naturally with his arm and took the leg bail of our number six batsman. We were in real trouble, and for the next hour and a half I enjoyed a splendid struggle with Archie Smith. I got

116

the better of him, not without a fair share of luck, and by the end of the day I had scored an undefeated sixty and we had won by a couple of wickets.

It was great fun and the Gorran players were generous in their praise and asked me whether I would play for them next season. I told them I would have to wait and see what happened, but if I moved in the Gorran direction I would very much like to join them. In the meantime, I must naturally continue with St Austell.

In the early part of July my parents came down. My mother was fascinated by Willie Rollins and his quaint manner. I took my father out on one of the few reasonably fine days. He sat in the bows with an uncle of mine and watched us work. They were clearly interested and slightly amazed; I suppose, not unnaturally. Neither my parents nor Biddie's mother at any time asked us whether we intended doing this for a lifetime, but I had little doubt that they were concerned; they wisely kept their counsel and gave us their tacit support. I always regret that I did not know Biddie's father. I saw him for a moment when we were engaged to be married; he died before our wedding day. During this brief meeting—for he was too ill for me to stay more than a few minutes—I saw a man full of character and heard a voice that was cultured and deeply rich in tone, so often associated with men who have known the deep seas. He was a fruit-grower in the Vale of Evesham, but before this he had spent five years of his life before the mast.

We had another visitor that summer. He had come for a quiet time, but it didn't turn out that way. His name was Bill Barnet and we had both served together in the Mediterranean, sharing the discomforts of the Sicily and Italy landings—in particular, Salerno and Anzio. He was big and jovial and had a booming voice.

Just before he arrived I had bought a very old red Morgan three-wheeler for £90. The first time out, I was driving Biddie proudly towards Fowey when the front axle broke. We had begun our long experience of second-hand cars. It had been repaired by the time Bill arrived and I showed him the three-wheeler with pride.

The following day I took Bill out in the *Coral* and he had a taste of spiltering. He stuck it well, but found it upset his stomach when the boat was riding to the line. This was always the testing time, and if people survived this slithering motion they could call themselves good sailors. Bill, like Biddie, was a help in the boat, for he would steer, leaving me free to concentrate on baiting my line. In harbour he would stand alongside me and help clear the line, or I would send him off to get the fuel.

One evening we returned home to find an answer from a letter we had written to a woman who bred Labradors in South Molton, Devon. We had written asking if she possessed a Labrador puppy of about four months who was broad-headed, thick-chested and intelligent. She replied in her letter that she had just the dog, and would we go over that week-end, preferably Saturday. The father and mother were Banchories and the price was twelve guineas. We wrote back at once and said that we would be over soon after lunch on Saturday.

So at ten o'clock that Saturday we set off in our 1929 three-wheeler for South Molton. Biddie, as the smallest of us, sat in the not very comfortable back. We jogged along and after an hour pulled in for some petrol. Unfortunately, I had forgotten to bring my petrol coupons, but the garage proprietor kindly gave us what we wanted after we had promised to send him on the coupons.

We made very poor headway and several times had to stop and fix the lead on to one or the other of the two plugs that stuck out of the old twin-cylinder engine. At last, much later than we had intended, we came in sight of South Molton, a dreamy Devonshire village. But our troubles were not over, for before we had actually reached South Molton the Morgan began to slither from side to side.

"Puncture," roared Bill Barnet. And I stopped the machine and we all climbed out.

"We'll have to push it," said Bill rather obviously. In this state we arrived in South Molton, tired and badly in need of a wash. The only garage would not touch it until Sunday morning. There was nothing for it but to spend the night here. We had nothing with us and very little money. We managed to convince the manager of the little grey-stone hotel that we were not undesirables, though it took a little doing, and we signed our names and had a wash. After tea we hired a taxi and went out to see the puppy.

The old car we had hired wandered down the narrow twisting lanes, flanked by high hedges, till we came to a low, gracious house, overlooking a terraced lawn. There was no gate or enclosure, simply the house and the lawn, open to the lane.

"Here you are," said the taxi-man, and we asked him to pick us up in an hour's time.

We got out and heard deep barks, followed by sharp ones. Round a corner of the house came two full-grown Labradors and half a dozen puppies. They jumped around our legs, and a lady came over and talked to us.

"There's yours," she said, and Biddie bent down and stroked the puppy. There was little doubt that he was going to be a big dog; his paws and head were enormous, but he seemed terribly shy.

We all went inside the house, and sat in a long, low room, in one corner of which stood a full-sized grand piano. Through the windows, which reached almost to the floor, we could see the puppies gambolling outside.

"They've never been inside a house," she said. "We've given them milk and the paunches of rabbits."

It was dark inside the room and very quiet and I could hear mice in the wainscoting. We talked of Labradors and she told us about this gracious old house in which she lived.

"We have no electricity," she added, and somehow it seemed natural that this house should be lit by the soft glow of lamps and candles.

The taxi arrived and we got up to go. I gave her a cheque for our pup, and we shook hands.

"We'll be over about ten o'clock tomorrow to pick him up, if that's all right," and we waved goodbye to her.

On Sunday morning we all three had a good breakfast, Bill and I in a washed but unshaven condition. We said goodbye to the proprietor and went to the garage, where our back tyre had actually been repaired.

The noise of that three-wheeler was rude and loud and it seemed wrong that South Molton should be so disturbed this Sunday morning. The dogs and puppies were out on the lawn and the lady was waiting for us. We got out and walked over the grass and up a small bank to where they were playing. Kim, for this was the name we had decided on, seemed the odd man out. He was bigger than the others and quieter. As we stood watching, he was accidently knocked down the bank by two of the other puppies, who were busy fighting. His legs seemed to go from under him and he let out a high-pitched squeal as he rolled down the bank. Biddie went and picked him up and the lady handed me his pedigree. We all shook hands and got back into the Morgan.

Kim was plainly very frightened at the sound of the engine, but he lay quite still, never attempting to move. Biddie stroked his ears and I think he knew he was in safe hands.

The church bell was ringing and the villagers were on their way to Sunday morning service as we finally left South Molton.

Our journey home ranks as one of our more difficult car journeys, though not the worst. Bill started the ball rolling by examining the map and suggesting we took a short cut. It was, of course, no short cut and, apart from getting hopelessly lost, we nearly lost our lives at one point. "Steep Hill"—read the notice and I dropped into low gear. We seemed to gather speed as we approached a corner.

"Put your brakes on," roared Bill.

"They are full on," I shouted to him above the noise of the engine.

"Take it wide. Take it wide," he boomed. What he meant I'm not sure.

We swung round the corner, to see the road dip even more steeply down to a few cottages and then rise almost perpendicularly on the other side. A farm-hand was walking slowly up the hill towards us. He leapt wildly to the side of the road as we careered down this steep incline. I saw several people staring in amazement at us as we passed the cottages and shot up the other side of the hill. Suddenly I realised our chain was off, and we came to a stop halfway up. At once we began to go backwards.

"Stop her," shouted Bill.

"Hold on," I cried and I swung her stern first into the hedge before she gathered any more speed.

We all got out, and I saw several people at the bottom of the hill looking up at us. We guided the three-wheeler down to the bottom, where two farm-hands, seeing our difficulty, fetched some tools and very kindly helped us put on the chain. We thanked them with warmth, for they might well have been most hostile after our outrageous piece of motoring, and set off once again.

During this repair Kim had not been very helpful, for every time Biddie had put him on the ground he had simply sat and shivered, whimpering a little and refusing to move. Looking over my shoulder at him now, as he lay as quiet as a lamb on Biddie's lap, I wondered if he was always going to be as frightened and docile as he had so far shown himself to be. It was, of course, not a fair test to expect him to enjoy this car trip, but he had looked a timid creature on the lawn that morning. Perhaps he had sensed that he was leaving his brothers and sisters and was sad at the prospect.

By half-past two we were in familiar country and only had fifteen more miles to cover. I had had to drive very carefully, using the engine as a brake, for there was very little response when I used the brake pedal. It had begun to rain and the three-wheeler had no hood. It was now that our last mishap occurred when we were going up a hill. The throttle was on the steering wheel and I used my thumb and forefinger to operate it. Suddenly, as I pushed it wide open with my thumb, the wire parted and the cable hung loose. I passed the wire casing quickly to Bill.

"Pull the wire, Bill," I called and at once the engine, which had nearly been stalling, picked up and we got to the top of the hill.

"Easy, easy, Bill," I said, and he pushed the wire in and our speed decreased.

"Bit of a hill coming up, Bill. Give her the gun," and he pulled feverishly at the wire and the three-wheeler sped up the hill.

"Slow her down," and he obliged by poking in the wire again, and so we proceeded in this mad-cap fashion, drenched with rain and thoroughly uncomfortable, until eventually we reached Mevagissey and home.

"I came down for a quiet holiday and I got landed with this," boomed Bill over his cup of tea, and he laughed so loud that Kim, in fear, disgraced himself.

Bill stayed with us another week, and amongst the many useful jobs he did, none was more appreciated than the worming of Kim. From that day on Kim filled out and never looked back. But it was several weeks before he would go out far from the house on a walk. We never had him on the lead and he always followed, keeping close in at our heels. He was terrified of other dogs and would stand with his tail between his legs, ears back, petrified with fear, while his friends and enemies sniffed around him. He would follow Biddie from room to room and liked always to be with one of us. Gradually as the weeks passed he grew more confident, and looked every inch a thoroughbred, with his great head and deep chest. He was still frightened of other dogs, for he had not, as yet, realised his full strength. He was splendid company and we were both delighted with him and he with us.

The spiltering season was nearly over. August had come and gone and the weather had been bad throughout the month and the fish far from plentiful. One day in the last week of August we were out spiltering when a thick fog descended upon us. It was as if there were just the three of us alone in a white world. We were in the shipping lanes and a foghorn was blowing persistently and with increasing power somewhere away on our port side.

"Get out the fog-horn, Sam," said George. Sam got it out of our forecastle and handed it to him. George put it between his lips and blew a long blast. He was pulling the line at the time, but had now stopped to listen. He blew again and again and then listened. There was a ship very close by.

"Here," he said and handed me the fog-horn. I wanted to lean over and dip the mouth piece in the sea and cleanse it of George's tobacco spittle. But I had neither the courage nor the time.

"Blow it," he roared, and I blew, making a noise not unlike a child blowing a trumpet at a Christmas party. A great blast of a foghorn replied.

"Bloody close," murmured Sam and I gave another answering squawk. Again came a great blast, but this time from our starboard side. The ship had passed us, but we had not seen her. Out of the whiteness around us the wash of the unseen ship came at us and rocked us quietly. We looked at each other, continued work, and no one spoke.

We came back that afternoon entirely by compass and clock. After we had run three and a quarter hours, we shut down the Kelvin and Sam went forward and peered ahead. We continued for some ten minutes, going very slowly. The water was flat calm and everything in the boat glistened with the wet. Sometimes we passed a gull, which would loom up like a cliff as it sat quietly on the water.

"Rocks," shouted Sam.

"Stop her," said George. Out of the fog we could see we were right under great cliffs.

"We're to the south of Mevagissey," George decided and we motored slowly north, parallel to the coast and right in under the cliffs.

We had been going for some fifteen minutes and I could see that George was far from happy. Suddenly there was a slight rift in the fog and I saw George studying the cliffs in great detail.

"That's the Black Head," he muttered and we turned round and retraced our steps. He was quite right and in twenty minutes we had picked up Mevagissey Light. We had not been on the southern side of Mevagissey at all, but were to the north.

One day during the early part of September I met the Reverend Henry Kendall, who was Headmaster of St Edward's School, Oxford. He had been a boy and master at my old school, Shrewsbury, and he now came forward with a splendid offer. He had heard that I was fishing down here and someone had also told him that we had got to move out of our present house by the end of September. He asked me whether we would like to go into his cottage at Portmellon.

"You can have it for five shillings a week, but I must warn you," he added, "that it's a wild place in the winter."

I jumped at this wonderful offer, and he told me he would be out by the end of the second week of September and we could go in when we liked. This was good news indeed, and the following week-end he kindly invited us over to tea and showed us the house.

Three days later George Pearce left us. We had been out fishing in bad weather. The wind was south-east and strong and there was a steep sea running as we neared home. On the way we passed a naval frigate proceeding slowly and rolling heavily. I saw Sam watching her closely. It must have brought back memories to him, for he had just completed twenty-three years in the Service.

We came alongside and tied up. Suddenly, without a

word of warning, George seized his tin of food, lowered himself over the side into the *Babs* and pulled himself ashore by means of the painter. He never turned, but simply walked away and disappeared up a turning.

Sam and I looked at each other. "What's up with George?" he asked.

"No idea," I replied. "But I think he's finished with us," and I was right.

We continued baiting-up our lines in silence, and I wondered what this new turn of events would mean. At first I was very worried, for the fishermen had taken great trouble to find a good man for us and now we had gone and lost him.

But gradually it became clear to me that there was not a great future for George if he stayed with us. The spiltering season was over and some of the boats had already hauled their nets aboard and were out chasing the pilchards. Besides, George had taught us a great deal about lining, and I suddenly felt I'd like to finish the week spiltering by ourselves. It would be interesting to see if we could do the job without the aid of a professional.

We finished baiting our lines and took George's three tubs ashore. When we were satisfied that the *Coral* was all ship-shape we went ashore, having agreed to meet at two-fifteen the following morning.

I told Biddie when I got home that George Pearce had suddenly and without a word left us.

"What an extraordinary thing," she said. "I am sorry, because I liked George, and I shall miss his scallops."

125

I stroked Kim's head while I told her of our plans to see the week out on our own.

"Can you manage?" she asked. "I'd love to come with you, but we can't very well leave Kim by himself for all that time." I agreed entirely, and added that it was time we had a go at it ourselves.

We didn't do badly for the rest of the week. We both knew what had to be done and, although we were slow, we shot and hauled our line and caught a few fish. I shot the line while Sam pushed the tubs into position. We took it in turns hauling the line. On our first day on our own we caught four baskets of whiting, two baskets of dogs and a few ray and ling and four fine turbot. We had done as well as the others, even if we were the last to finish.

Sam was a good companion and a most methodical worker, but he was still very slow at baiting-up and pulling a line. Looking back on it all, he did well, for at forty-one to attempt to make a living in a job which required nimble fingers and deftness of movement was asking a lot. As I watched him, I could see that he would never get any faster. He pulled the line slowly and he seemed to make three separate movements in clearing the line. First he would get hold of the fish, next unhook the creatures and lastly drop them into the fish-berth. Through no fault of his own, he would never get much faster, and he wisely went his own pace. But I was several times sorely tempted to call out to him :

"Come on, Sam. Let's hurry up and get the bloody thing inboard !"

Friday was our last day of spiltering, and as we motored slowly back to the eastern dan, I noticed a great bank of black clouds massing to the south-east.

"Take a look over there, Sam," I called out to him.

"Doesn't look too good," he replied. I glanced around us. All the boats looked as though they were getting their lines fast.

"Best get to work quickly," I said, and we both agreed.

126

As I hauled the creeper up I could feel the wind growing colder, and there was no doubt we were in for a blow. I pulled the line hard for an hour and then handed over to Sam. We weren't catching many fish and perhaps it was as well, for the weather was getting worse. After a while I again took over from Sam, and eventually we had the line all inboard, and not before time. I started up the Kelvin and then we turned and ran helter-skelter for home, driven forward by a south-east gale. Whenever a bigger sea ran down on our port quarter we would ease the *Coral* away in the same direction as the wave, like a boxer riding a punch, and then bring her back on course again.

We approached the harbour and saw that the coastguard station had hoisted a black cone, indicating an easterly gale warning.

As we passed Mevagissey Light, I looked back for a second at the dark sky and grey, sullen sea, flecked by white horses, and suddenly I felt glad that we were in and this was Friday and the spiltering season had ended.

I stopped for a moment before going home and looked at the harbour.

The summer was over. The boats were straining at their moorings before the rising gale. Against the dark sky a few gulls, their cries carried away on the wind, swooped down on the defenceless luggers. I stood a moment longer, quite lost in the full enjoyment of this scene before I turned and walked home.

KIM

CHAPTER EIGHT

Catherine and Football

AT the end of the second week of September we moved again, this time to Portmellon, transferring our chattels once more by taxi. I had sold our three-wheeler just before this move, after it had played its most annoying trick to date on me: it caught fire. I had cranked the little beast for a considerable time before she would start and then, as though in disgust at my efforts, smoke began to appear from under the dashboard. I immediately stopped the engine and then rather stupidly dabbed with a rag somewhere behind the dashboard. This was ineffective and I only succeeded in touching a red-hot wire and burning my fingers. Eventually the smoke stopped after I had disconnected the battery. But I had had enough by now, and I promptly advertised the Morgan for sale. She went for seventy pounds—twenty pounds less than we had given—and neither of us was sorry to see her go.

Our new house was quite different from anything we had previously experienced. It was in the middle of a row of four attached houses, facing the sea, within twelve yards of the beach. The main entrance, protected by a glass portico, led on to a concrete front shielded from the road by a low wall. On the other side of the road was a thick four-foot wall against which, at high water, the seas would crash in bad weather, flinging sheets of spray and pebbles and sometimes solid water across the road and on to our row of four houses. In such conditions the road was quite impassable for the odd cars that attempted the passage at such a time.

This row of four houses lay at the top of a natural little

inlet a mere fifty yards wide. They faced south-east, and we never wearied of looking out at this narrow stretch of water, girt by its rocky cliffs on which a half-dozen cottages on the north side perched precariously, their walls as grey and weathered as their foundations.

Almost adjoining our row of houses were Mitchell's boat-building sheds. I spent many hours watching the "chippies" at work and I never ceased to wonder how Percy Mitchell could produce such fine boats from such ramshackle sheds. Percy Mitchell was a large, heavy man, slow of movement and speech. His words were always to the point and seemed to come from somewhere deep down inside him, and he had a slow, winning smile. He seemed to me as solid as the great balks of timber stacked around him.

The other boat-builder was Will Frazer of Mevagissey. Physically he was quite different from Percy Mitchell, being slight of build and quick of movement. He had a keen sense of humour and his face, which was full of lines, would crease when he smiled. It was easy to tell whether a boat was built by Percy Mitchell or Will Frazer by studying the characteristics of the boats. Percy's boats were like himself, solid, fine, bilgy boats, with a good beam and bluff bows. Will's boats were slighter and more pretty to look at, with fine, slender bows and a shapely stern which gave them a good turn of speed. They both built splendid boats and were craftsmen at their work.

We had lots of room in our new house, which was really no more than a holiday home; indeed, this was what Mr Kendall used it for. In the summer he would bring down parties of boys from his school and pack them away inside the house like sardines.

Peter Husband lived on the north side of the cove, just up the road in one of the cottages perched on top of the cliff. On the southern side of Percy Mitchell's yard the road bent sharply and soared up Bodrugan Hill, where it became very steep at the top before swinging first to the left and then to the right. The walk into Mevagissey along the top of the cliffs took a good fifteen minutes, and we were never tired of doing it. One started uphill from Portmellon, then went along a quarter of a mile of flat but twisting road, before one reached the top of Polkirt Hill, which plunged precipitously down into Mevagissey village. The Black Head and Fowey Light, the latter so often sunlit, were a magnet to the eye and a never-ending source of pleasure to us both.

Kim, too, loved the walk into Mevagissey, except when he reached the top of Polkirt Hill. Twenty yards before he came to this spot, he would begin to lag behind and walk in a zigzag and dejected fashion. The reason for this was that on our very first walk he had been attacked by a large brown shaggy-coated mongrel. Kim had promptly sat on his haunches and let forth shriek upon shriek of anguish. The brown dog had not bitten, but simply growled ferociously and reared up at him. We drove the brown dog off and I picked up Kim and carried him into the field that runs down towards the outer harbour. Every time Kim walked past this spot at the top of Polkirt Hill—and Biddie took him into Mevagissey most days—the brown dog was waiting. One day we decided it was too absurd for Kim to behave any longer in this fashion, much as we sympathised with him.

"Let's walk on," I told Biddie, "and see what happens. He's quite big enough to look after himself now, and if it develops into a fight we'll separate them at once."

Once again we reached the spot, and there was the brown dog advancing menacingly down the steps of his home. I glanced quickly over my shoulder at Kim, who had stopped and waited with his ears flat and his tail hanging limply. He watched us with mute sadness and unbelief as we callously walked ahead. I could hear the snarl of the brown dog increasing in tempo and ferocity.

"Come on, boy," I called to Kim. And we walked on wondering what was going to happen. Suddenly there was a new terrible roaring sound and, turning quickly, we were in time to see Kim rear up and knock the brown dog clean off his feet. Without waiting to push home his attack, he bounded towards us in great leaps. With every hair of his coat standing on end, he leapt at us and leapt again in sheer joy and then, as though it were time he regained his dignity, he walked ahead with a light step and a jaunty spring. Never again did the brown dog go near him, for Kim had found his manhood.

Sam and I had begun netting again, and it was a joy to handle a pilchard net after those hundreds of little hooks. We had only put seven nets aboard, for we considered this a sufficient number to begin the season. One night, as we lay to our nets, we discussed the question of shipping another hand.

"What about asking George Allen?" I suggested.

"Well, he's not working at the moment, I know," said Sam. "Personally, I think it would be a good idea."

The following day I saw George Allen walking along the outer harbour quay and at once went out to meet him.

"Morning, George," I greeted him.

"Morning, me dear," he answered softly, smiling and drawing heavily on his cigarette. He was wearing his black suit and black beret. He still looked just as crafty as ever, I thought, as his brown eyes peered up at me through his steel-rimmed glasses. I thought of our first meeting in Dartmouth and I couldn't help smiling.

"What's funny?" he asked.

Good old George, I thought with warmth, and I asked him there and then if he would like to come and ship along with us for the pilchard season.

He took a last long drag at his cigarette, making a slight hissing sound as he took the smoke deep down into his lungs. I waited for his reply while he flicked his cigarette into the water and emitted a long cloud of smoke.

"All right, me dear. When shall we be going out? Tonight?"

"Yes," I replied.

"Good. The sooner the better. What time shall I be down?"

"About four-thirty," I told him.

We walked back together and he was obviously pleased to join us.

That afternoon George was aboard the *Coral* again. I let him take her out of the harbour, and as I watched him peering ahead after the other boats, I thought of our first night out together and how near we had been to disaster. But this time I had no qualms and George made no attempt to go in a different direction from the fleet. He was good company in the boat and I enjoyed these nights on the water as October came and went.

About this time, Robert, Biddie's brother, wrote and offered to give us his little 1932 M.G. We were both thrilled, and one week-end went up to Evesham to fetch it. We got a great deal of fun out of the little car, but its engine was really finished, for the car had been owned by a number of R.A.F. officers and finally by Robert himself, who had also been a Flight Lieutenant in the R.A.F.

Early in October I played my first match for Mevagissey in the Junior Football League of Cornwall. The Mevagissey football ground lay above the village, situated in a very rough and sloping field with magnificent views of the sea and coast to the north. I had been elected captain, which I considered a great honour. How this was decided and who had been responsible for the decision I never found out. No one had seen me play, and though I had played for Shrewsbury School for two seasons, nobody knew of this. Even if they had known this fact, it would have meant nothing to a Cornish fishing village.

My recollections of my days playing for Mevagissey are hazy, but several events and one personality in particular stand out clearly.

Catherine was her name, and she was a great supporter of mine. She would sit at her upstairs window overlooking the corner of the harbour by Williams's engineering shop, and watch the fishermen as they went in and out. She lived for her football and hated to see the Mevagissey side lose, which I'm afraid they did rather too often. Around the touch-line on this appalling yet beautiful football pitch, twenty or thirty fishermen would be grouped. They would stand talking and shouting ribald encouragement. Major Barton, the Chairman, who was as responsible as anyone for keeping the club going, would stand a little apart and periodically shout, "Well played, Mevagissey."

But the person who really stole the limelight was Catherine, who would stand in the middle and shout her own form of encouragement on these lines.

"Come on, Charlie, me old dear. You'm show 'em. Well played! Ooh, you dirty bastard! Yes, you'm did. I saw you. Referee! referee!" and here she would advance on to the pitch, egged on by the supporters. "Why don't you stop him, ref, and blow your bloody whistle?" I have always been amused by the comments of male football supporters, but never particularly by women. Catherine, however, was an exception. Perhaps it was that Junior League football in Cornwall has a quality all of its own, and to me Catherine was part of the setting. Whatever the weather, there she would be, exhorting her side with a running commentary, delivered with such amusing emphasis and conviction that in spite of the ferocity of her criticism, I for one could never feel any annoyance at her antics.

One day, however, she went almost too far. The match had been a particularly tough one and we'd gone down with all colours flying. When the final whistle blew Catherine was ready. With a huge lump of mud, she ran at the referee and I saw it go sailing past his head. Not content at her near-miss, she aimed a kick at his backside. But the referee did not stay for more, and Catherine was left disconsolate and angry in the middle of the muddy field.

"Come on, Catherine," I said. "We'll win the next match for you."

"You'm played a wonderful game, me old beauty," she

said. "Yes, you'm did. A really wonderful game," and together we walked off the field.

But the matter did not end there, for the Committee had observed Catherine's attack and felt, I think rightly, that something had to be done to protect referees on the Mevagissey football ground from any further assaults of this kind. However, the action they took was too fierce and poor Catherine was banned from watching any more matches.

The following week we played away, but the week after I found myself once again spinning a coin on that wonderful but impossible football pitch. The game had not been in progress for more than a few minutes when I noticed a commotion going on in the hedge that ran up one side of the pitch. The spectators had turned their heads—indeed, all eyes, including the players', were watching the hedge, which was moving about and from which strange noises were coming.

Suddenly it burst asunder and with a shout of triumph Catherine emerged. There was laughter all round, but Catherine wasted no time: "Come on, me old dears. You show 'em how to play. Go on, Alf! Oh, you dirty devil! Yes, you did. You did it on purpose. Referee. . . ." And so it went on until the end of the game. On this occasion her cup was full, for it was one of the few games we won that season.

Another time we played somewhere inland with snow lying thick on the ground and an icy east wind blowing the full length of the pitch. We were two goals down at half-time and changed ends to face the biting wind. They were a better side than we were, and I found we were well and truly up against it. Of a sudden I felt there was something wrong, and I was right, for our left back had decided he'd had enough and was already halfway to the small wooden shed where we had changed. I pulled back one of our inside forwards to wing half and sent the wing half to left back. Within minutes the right back had decided he'd had enough and was already running towards the wooden shed. The wind shrieked in mockery and the cold was an agony. Our opponents scored twice quickly, and to my utter amazement I suddenly saw our outside right sprint rapidly from the pitch and make a bee-line for the shed. There was now a very definite wavering in the ranks, and suddenly we all ran for it, as hard as we could, straight for the wooden shed, where some relief from the cruel wind awaited us. I was roaring with laughter by the time I had reached the door. But I didn't laugh for long, for hard on our heels were our opponents, followed by their supporters, a very angry-looking crowd indeed. I nipped inside quickly, and not a moment too soon.

There was a loud banging on the door and a furious voice asked us what the hell we thought we were doing.

"Tell 'em to go to hell," came the helpful advice from Billy More, who was already changing.

I opened the door and cautiously looked out.

"Are you going to finish the game or are you going to give us the points?" demanded their captain with considerable anger.

"Certainly you may have the points," I replied, and that was the end of that match.

But they were happy and intensely amusing football matches. Later on when I was captain of the Oxford University football side, I brought the team down to play two matches against Cornwall. We won both our matches, and a good number of the fishermen came to watch us. I took the team over to Mevagissey and introduced them to the fishermen.

"He'm never could do any bloody good for us," said Edgar when I introduced him to Donald Carr, the Derbyshire cricket captain.

"No, and he's not much good for us," agreed Donald with a laugh.

In 1951 I was to find myself at Wembley Stadium playing centre-half for Pegasus against Bishop Auckland, before a crowd of 100,000. We won 2—1. Two years later we were at Wembley again before another 100,000 crowd, and this time we beat Harwich and Parkeston 6–0. I now had two gold Cup-winner's medals and many telegrams from well-wishers, two of which I was delighted to see were from Mevagissey Football Club and Gorran Cricket Club.

We saw a good deal of Peter Husband, and when the wind blew strongly from the wrong quarter, he would come and help us put up our outside shutters.

"Better batten her down tonight," he would say. "There's plenty of wind coming in from the east."

Suddenly he would jump at Kim, who would stand patiently watching us preparing for the coming storm. This would frighten the dog and make him move quickly away with tail drooping. Peter always did this to Kim, and then he would stand and call to him in a puzzled voice, "Come here, you silly old man," but apparently he could never understand why Kim would not go near him.

"Funny," he would say. "He seems frightened of me." In the evenings he would often drop in and see us, sometimes bringing a suitable bone.

It was all really most embarrassing, for Kim would at once move over to either my chair or Biddie's. Nothing on earth would persuade him to go near Peter with his tempting bone.

"Come on, old boy," Peter would call, but Kim would not move. All the time we knew Peter, and we saw a lot of him while at Portmellon, Kim would never go near him. Frankly, Peter had only himself to blame, for he would jump boisterously at the dog whenever he saw him outside. But I have never seen anything so dignified and quietly pointed as the way Kim would immediately arise on the arrival of Peter Husband and, as discreetly as possible, disappear out of sight behind one of our chairs.

October and November had passed and December was well under way. The weather had been fine and we had spent many happy nights on the water, though without notable success. On fine evenings Biddie would come out with us, and as we lay to our nets a boat would sometimes hail us and ask us what the football side's prospects were for the following Saturday. In the early hours of the morning, the time varying according to what we had caught, I would climb into the M.G. and drive through the sleeping village, up Polkirt Hill, along the top of the cliffs, before turning down to Portmellon. If Peter Husband happened to finish at the same time as ourselves, then I would give him a lift home in the M.G.

We had decided to go to London before Christmas and stay with Robbie, an old naval friend, for a couple of nights, before going down to our respective parents for a few days. I had told Sam and George that we should be away over Christmas for a week and that he and George could carry on fishing and generally look after the boat in my absence.

On 22 December at seven o'clock on a dark and freezing morning we left Portmellon, bound for London. I had strapped our two green naval suitcases on to the small luggage rack on the back of the M.G. There was very little room inside the two-seater and Biddie consequently had to have Kim on her knee. He was heavy, but he did at least keep her warm. Although we had side-screens to the car, they were far from draught-proof, which did not add to the comfort of the journey. We took the south road to Exeter, going through Lostwithiel, Liskeard, Tavistock. Once through Exeter we picked up the London road, and then began our misfortunes. It was freezing hard and the roads were icy. Into the bargain, our clutch had begun to slip. We were well behind schedule and I was anxious to press on, but a stop was now inevitable.

"Nothing much we can do for you," said the garage mechanic. "Going far?"

"London," I replied.

"Bad forecast," he observed and, just to rub it in, he added for good measure: "It's freezing all over the country and there's snow coming."

"Well, what's the answer to this problem?" I asked him. He examined the clutch.

"Never was any good on this model. Trouble is you've got oil in your clutch plates," he added.

We waited patiently, resigned to the fact that the whole matter was out of our hands.

"I'll flush it out with petrol and that should take you on a bit," he suggested.

We thanked him, paid him and pushed on once again. Just before we reached Wincanton a car passed us with horn blowing while the passenger in the front seat leant out and pointed hard at us. Feeling there was something wrong, I stopped and got out.

At once I saw what they were trying to indicate to us. One of our suitcases had fallen off and the second one was only just hanging on. The rope had parted and I cursed myself for using cord that wasn't man enough for the job. I secured the remaining case and, turning the car round, retraced our steps for some ten miles, but we saw no sign of the suitcase.

Very depressed, we turned the car again and went back to Wincanton, where we enquired where the police station was. To find it we had to go down a very steep hill and promptly skidded, for the roads were now treacherous.

The police station was warm, but the police sergeant took a long while taking down my statement. I told him that we'd lost a green naval suitcase somewhere between Wincanton and a garage just outside Exeter, where we had stopped to have our clutch temporarily repaired.

Inside the case I told him were my wife's clothes, her jewellery and, for some unknown reason, her engagement ring. Slowly and laboriously he wrote it all down and then asked particulars about the ring.

"Well," he said, "we'll notify all the police stations and keep our eyes open. Where will you want the case sent to, if it's found?"

I gave him our Evesham address and, wishing him a happy Christmas, we both left.

Once outside, I thought it would be as well to check up

on the other suitcase and see that it was properly secure. Suddenly, as I started to do this, it dawned on me that it might well be my suitcase that had dropped off and not the one containing Biddie's possessions. We had naturally, though stupidly, in the anxiety of the moment, assumed at once that it was her case, with valuables inside, that had fallen.

With numb fingers I untied the knots as quickly as I could and opened the remaining suitcase. It was Biddie's.

"I shall have to go in again," I said to Biddie after I had told her the news, "and tell the police sergeant." I didn't look forward to this interview.

"I'm so sorry," I said as I stood once again before the police sergeant, "but I've been a complete fool and assumed that the case that fell off was my wife's. In actual fact it is my case that's missing."

He looked at me for quite a long time and it was clear he either doubted my sanity, or thought I was pulling his leg.

"Very well," he said at length. "We'll try again," and once more he began the slow business of getting out paper and pencil and taking down a list of what was inside my suitcase.

I thanked him again and moved towards the door.

"Are you sure you've not lost your missus now?" he asked with a slow smile.

"No," I replied. "She's sitting in the car, guarded by a big black dog."

But I was wrong, for there was no sign of Biddie or Kim when I got outside. However, I soon found her having a cup of tea just up the road, and promptly ordered one for myself.

We started out again, the time being half-past four in the afternoon. We still had one hundred and eleven miles to go, and the roads were so icy it was dangerous to go any faster than thirty miles an hour. We stopped twice to have our clutch cleaned out with petrol. It was dark now and we had to use our headlights. I used them as sparingly as possible, for the dashboard indicated a slight discharge and the battery was dying on us.

On and on we went, cramped and cold, wondering whether we ever would reach our destination that night.

At 10.15 we had reached the Kingston by-pass, when the car stopped completely. The petrol gauge was very low, but I thought there was enough in the tank to reach Sutton. However, I at once assumed that we were out of petrol. Across the road was a pub with a taxi outside. I hurried across and went into the public bar. Discreetly I enquired whether the owner of the taxi was present.

"Yes, mate. What do you want?" said a voice on my right.

"I wonder if you could help me and run me to a garage to get a drop of petrol. I've come up from Cornwall and I'm out of juice and have got to get across to Sutton," I explained.

"Sorry, mate," he said. "I've finished for the night."

"Well, thank you," I said and started to go towards the door.

"What's your trouble?" a voice called out.

"I'm out of petrol," I replied. "And I've been motoring since seven o'clock from Mevagissey."

"Here," he said. "Take my keys. In the back of my black Morris, you'll find a two-gallon drum. Help yourself."

"It's very kind of you," I told him, "and I'm really more grateful than I can say."

"By the way," he added, "do you know the Ship Inn at Mevagissey?"

"I do indeed," I replied.

"Do you know that wonderful character—George Pearce?"

"I know him very well. He fished with me all through the summer."

"Give him my regards when you return," said this stranger.

"I certainly will," I told him and went out and put some of his petrol in the M.G.

I gave him back his keys and we had a quick drink together and then I left. I never knew who he was and I never saw him again, but it was a warm gesture.

There was just a flicker of life left in the battery as I swung her. I cranked her solidly for five minutes without a suggestion of a cylinder firing. I realised it could not have been the petrol after all. But surely, I thought, there's enough life left in the battery to get her going and do these last ten or twelve miles.

"It's no good, Biddie," I called to her. "I'm afraid we shan't reach Sutton tonight. We shall have to try and find somewhere to spend the night."

We sat for a moment in the tiny two-seater, chilled to the bone, cramped, tired and hungry. We had been on the road for fifteen and a half hours and we'd had enough. Kim too had found it very cramped, but he had been wonderfully patient under the most trying circumstances. I stroked his great head.

It was all very quiet and there were no cars on the road. Suddenly we heard footsteps crunching the frozen snow underfoot. Then a most extraordinary thing happened to us.

We heard a voice call out: "Are you in trouble?"

We both got out and there was a man and his wife with their two young sons. They were all taking a last breath of fresh air before going to bed.

"Yes," I said. "Frankly, we are."

"What's your difficulty?" the man asked me, and I told him quickly the full story of our journey and how the battery had now finally died on us.

"Hop in," he said, after he had listened quietly to my story, "and we'll give you a push and see if she'll start."

Nothing happened and I got out again. I saw the man talking to his wife.

"Look," he said, "I can help you in two ways. Choose whichever one you like. We'll either put you up for the night or I'll tow you to Sutton."

"Good gracious!" we said after a slight pause. "We couldn't possibly ask you to do that."

"I shall be offended if you don't," he said, "and I shall expect you to choose the one which is most convenient to you both."

It was a fantastic offer, for it was eleven o'clock, the roads were icy, it was freezing hard and it was Saturday night.

"We'd love to get to Sutton tonight," I said tentatively.

"Splendid," said this astonishing person. "We'll go and get the car and I'll make out a piece of cardboard for an 'On Tow' sign to put on the back of your car."

In twenty minutes he was back and, having fixed up the tow, he took us gently to Sutton, to the very door of the house where Robbie lived.

We got out to thank him, a difficult task. I wanted at least to pay for his petrol, but he would not hear of it.

"Then please give your two boys this pound note for Christmas," I pleaded, and I thrust it upon him.

He thanked me and laughed, shook me by the hand and, before we had realised it, had got back into his car and driven away into the darkness and out of our lives. We stood listening to the noise of his engine as it quickly died away into the night. I wished I had found out his name and address but it was now too late. Perhaps he will read this book. I hope he does.

We saw both our families over Christmas, and the day before we set off for Cornwall the lost suitcase arrived. A postman had found it, six miles to the west of Wincanton, and had taken great trouble to do it up securely and send it promptly by passenger train to Evesham.

On the way home we had an electrical breakdown when going through Bristol and the car was temporarily repaired in a bus depot, but we had to stop the night, eventually finding a place at two o'clock in the morning.

We set off again on Saturday morning and had to race against time to reach St Austell before two o'clock, for I was due to play football for Mevagissey at half-past on the St

Austell football ground. We arrived with a quarter of an hour to spare and lost yet another match.

But it was nice to be home and Kim bounded with joy at the familiar haunts. The air felt fresh and clear as we leant over the sea-wall and caught the smell of sand and salt water, rock and sea-weed. That evening Peter Husband and his wife came over to see us. They wanted to hear all our news, and were particularly amused when we told them of the occasion we had attended a well-known night-club, and had been forced to leave Kim behind the counter with the attendant in charge of the hats and coats.

"Well," said Peter, "you've not missed much fishing. Sam and George went out a couple of times, but they didn't do much. I believe the Looe boats have been doing well, though. Next week the boats will be going to the north, probably up to the Rame."

"By the way," he added before he left, and with a twinkle in his eyes, "Will Rollins is nearly out of Woodbines." We all laughed, and I walked as far as the Black Cottage with Peter and his wife.

"See you in the morning," called Peter with a cheery wave of his hand. I waved back and jumped down on to the beach, where Kim had already bounded ahead, a dark shadow on the smooth, wet sand. It was Saturday night and it was good to be back.

CHAPTER NINE

A Night of Storm

THE New Year dawned stormy and cold, and there were few nights when we could safely go to bed without putting up the shutters on the outside of the house. In the mornings we would walk into Mevagissey, meeting various fishermen on the way and stopping for a chat.

"Is the missus going out tonight?" they would enquire.

"Hope so," Biddie would reply.

"Proper job, proper job. You'm take her, me old dear," they'd say to me. "You always catch fish when she's aboard the *Coral*."

Kim, too, had his friends and particular haunts on the walk. We noticed that the brown dog would retreat to the top of the steps leading up to his house, and stand stiffly watching us till we had passed. There was no doubt that Kim thoroughly enjoyed this moment of the walk and strutted arrogantly past with never a glance in the direction of his old enemy. Then, as though he could contain himself no longer, he would turn round and come back to us, sweeping the whole length of his body from side to side in his excitement and pleasure.

I noticed that whenever strange dogs now approached him, he would experience a fleeting moment of anxiety, when he would wrestle with his old fear and give every indication that he was about to put his tail between his legs and shriek. But after that momentary indecision, every hair from his head to his tail would stand on end and he really looked a magnificent animal. Kim was not a fighter—Labradors as a breed never are—but he would stand no

144

nonsense from another dog, and if attacked he would fight back. I never saw him worsted.

We both hate fights; in fact, I find them quite terrifying. But I think the most frightening dog-fight I ever experienced, and, on reflection, one of the funniest, happened a year later when I was an undergraduate living in Woodstock. There was one particularly bad-tempered and really savage black dog, a perfect menace to the town. He was kept locked up most of the time, which was more than likely a contributory cause of his wicked temper. If he escaped, a thing that happened all too often, he would attack without warning or reason, and he was no mean size.

One day Biddie and I were shopping in the town with Kim just ahead of us. Suddenly, from the back entrance of a house on the opposite side, this black dog dashed straight across the road and flung himself at Kim with savage ferocity. Kim struck back with a deep roar. The dog was brave, for there was no doubt that Kim was gradually getting the better of him, but, come what may, I could not separate them. In desperation, but with little effect, I grabbed hold of Kim's tail and pulled. Suddenly I was struck on the ear by a flying cauliflower. Amazed, I looked up to see that Biddie had thrown this particularly hard vegetable.

"What on earth did you do that for?" I asked in astonishment.

"You've no right to pull Kim's tail," she replied above the noise of the fight. "It's most undignified for him."

Too stupefied to think of a suitable reply, I watched her go forward and quickly separate the two dogs. What she said to them or how she did it, I do not know. In as dignified a manner as possible, I bent down and picked up the cauliflower and together we walked on home, away from the small gathering of incredulous onlookers who had watched this episode.

We had long ago come to the conclusion that our 1932 M.G. was too small for us, so with a certain amount of regret we decided to sell her. Shortly afterwards I saw a

Willys Jeep advertised for £189. I asked William if he would come with me that evening to St Austell to vet the car, and I was delighted when he said that he would be ready at half-past six. After a thorough examination, I bought the jeep, which had an iron roof, a wooden body and no doors. But her engine was sweet and her performance excellent, though the latter could not be said of her petrol consumption. What we particularly liked about this, our third vehicle was that we could put all our possessions into the back, including Kim, and we were all able to travel in comparative comfort. One of Percy Mitchell's men fixed on two doors for me, and we gave her a coat of dark blue paint.

In early January Ted Doust and his daughter arrived to take up residence in the house next door. He had been stage carpenter at the Stratford-on-Avon Memorial Theatre, and had bought this house at Portmellon with a view to taking in guests during the summer months. He was bent and asthmatical and would shuffle forward with a worried expression on his face. Jo, his daughter, on the other hand, was the exact opposite and never allowed her father's anxieties to rob her of her naturally cheerful disposition. She had two female wire-haired terriers which went with her everywhere.

Sometimes in the evenings father and daughter would come over for an hour. Ted would sit staring into the fire while Jo talked to Biddie, with the two terriers on her lap. Outside, if it was high water, the dull thud of the waves hitting the sea wall could be heard, followed by the quick patter of flying spray striking our shutters.

"Sounds bad," Ted would remark, turning his head and body slowly round in my direction. I hadn't the heart to tell him how much more serious a south-east gale on spring tides would be. But, of course, neither had we experienced a real storm in Portmellon. We had tasted wild days when the road was impassable for a short time, but never a full gale, roaring in from the south-east, when the seas, caught in the bottle neck of Portmellon, would rush up the cove and

146

smash against the wall protecting the road and our four houses.

Before he had moved in, Ted had had his house decorated from top to bottom in preparation for the coming season. Most afternoons he would come shuffling across and ask if we were going to sea that night.

"Think we can leave the shutters down tonight?" he would ask, breathing heavily.

"Oh, yes. I think we'll be all right tonight, Ted," I would reply, and he'd nod and, after a long glance out to sea, shuffle back to his house, looking perhaps just a little less worried.

In the latter part of January snow came, and with it intense cold. Our walk into Mevagissey we found even more enjoyable, for the coastline, capped by snow as far as the eye could see, stood out brilliantly in the clear sunlit mornings.

From the top of Polkirt Hill we looked down at the village. The snow lay thick on the decks of the boats and the roofs of the cottages, and the whole scene had a still quality of breathless enchantment. But it was cold that night on the water and we pulled the nets with plenty of vigour. The night was clear and freezing and the water black and uninviting. The cliffs stood out sharply with their white mantles and gave the appearance of being much nearer than they actually were.

Kim thrived on this weather and once jumped into a brook, breaking the ice. He was a magnificent water dog and was quite at home in a rough sea, though, strangely enough, he did not enjoy going out in the *Coral*. The snow continued, but the freezing wind went round to the east and the fishermen faced a long spell of inactivity.

We lit great fires in an endeavour to warm the house, supplementing our coal ration with any odd pieces of wood that we could find lying outside Percy Mitchell's yard. On one bitterly cold night we really went too far and took a six-foot baulk of timber which appeared to have been cast aside. Returning, we thrust it straight into the fire, and as it burned we gradually pushed it further in, till the whole six feet were burnt. Peter Husband looked in that night and roared with laughter at our enormous log sticking out into the hearth. Perhaps if the cold had persisted much longer Percy Mitchell might, if he had chanced to look through his window, have seen us dragging one of his newly-constructed boats as fuel for our sitting-room fire.

By now the roads in and out of Mevagissey were impassable to cars and lorries, and, since there were no trains, it was impossible to reach St Austell except on foot. But there was one car that could keep going and did so, and that was our jeep. I earned money by running people into St Austell and taking coal and food to houses in inaccessible positions. With the jeep's low gear-ratio and four-wheel drive there was no hill that we were not prepared to face. I carried a few sacks in the car in case we should slip, and there were times when I had to use them. Once we journeyed to Dartmoor to see what it looked like in these conditions. There were hardly any cars on the road and when we got to the Moor there were no cars at all. Dartmoor looked bleak yet magnificent, but it was a foolhardy journey to have made in such conditions and on reflection I am surprised we did not run into trouble.

The cold spell lasted nearly two weeks and we did not go to sea much during this time. The battleship H.M.S. *Howe* came and anchored in the bay for several days. I took Biddie and the Bartons out in the *Coral* to look at this great ship. As I circled her that wintry morning I nearly fouled my mizzen on her boom. We cruised around for a while looking at the cliffs, which stood out stark and black in contrast to the white landscape. For a moment, as I looked at the coast, I was carried back to an afternoon in 1942 when from beneath the forward canopy of H.M.S. *Foresight's* motor boat, I had first seen the great bastions of Scapa Flow. It had been on just such a day that our long journey from Devonport Barracks to Scapa Flow had ended by our climbing wearily up the Jacob's ladder and on to the iron deck, after experiencing the fury of the Pentland Firth.

We were at once made to fall into a line and stand to attention to await the First Lieutenant, who then came forward to welcome us.

"You are all candidates for a commission," he began without any further preamble, "and as such you will be expected to work longer, work harder and work better than anyone else aboard this ship. Right. Carry on," he said, turning to the Quartermaster, and left us to digest his words of welcome.

I looked again at the massive steel ship, at the ratings working on the upper deck, heard again the long, shrill wail of the Bosun's pipe and decided it was time to return to Mevagissey Harbour.

That Saturday, Mevagissey Football Club played H.M.S. *Howe's* football side on our frozen ground. We lost, in spite of Catherine's vociferous support, which greatly amused the ratings. After the match I was unable to prevent the whole of the *Howe's* team from jumping on to the jeep. We eventually moved off down to the harbour with fifteen aboard.

The *Coral* had originally been built as a crabber, and I had often been told by the fishermen, that what she wanted was a good strake around her. This would give her more freeboard and one would feel more inside the boat. Neither Percy Mitchell nor Will Frazer could do the job for me at once. It struck me that it would be a good idea to have it done right away while there was not much doing in the fishing. Frazer suggested that I should go and see Alfie Cloke, who was a shipwright and whose son played in the Mevagissey football side. That week he started and finished this job of putting a seven-inch strake around the *Coral*, scarfing a piece into her bow and building it up. He made a good job of it and the *Coral* looked an even finer boat.

At last the weather turned warmer and the great thaw began. It is always sad to see the crisp brightness of snow turn to the grey, dirty slush of a thaw. The very air itself loses its intoxication and the spirit wilts with the melting snow, until the colour and shape of the countryside become once more apparent. But this 1947 cold spell had lasted a long time and everyone welcomed the warmer weather.

For a week the boats fished hard around Par Bay and off the Gribbin. I remember one night particularly. We had all shot our nets in trots. The night was peaceful and warm and a boat over to starboard gave us a friendly hail across the water. The moon was in its first quarter as we lay for five hours waiting for the fish to go to net. Periodically we would haul in a few corbal strops, but there was nothing much going on. It was one o'clock in the morning when Sam, George and I all decided to pull the nets aboard. We hauled in all nine nets and shook out barely twenty stone of fish. We motored gently back and moored the *Coral* in the silent inner harbour. I walked home feeling at peace with the world. The moon had disappeared and there was no wind as I looked back towards the Black Head. There were several boats on their way in, their mast-head lights creeping over the dark water. I slowly walked home, the stillness of the night broken only by the singing of the telephone wires overhead and the beat of the distant engines as the boats returned to harbour.

Next morning I was amazed to see some of the crews still shaking out pilchards.

"You'm left too early last night, old man," said Willie Rollins.

"If you'd stayed another half an hour you'd have had a hundred stone of fish and more," added Edgar, who had just come up. "You be too keen on that bed of yours." He laughed. "Fish will often go to net like that soon after the moon goes down. Hey, Willie here wants a Woodbine," and they all laughed.

That afternoon the Old Black Hawk arrived. Why we called him that I'm not really sure, for there was certainly nothing hawklike about his appearance. I think it was the fact that we hadn't been in Mevagissey five minutes before he had swooped upon us trying to sell an insurance policy. He would call regularly and was never dismayed at my persistent refusals. Eventually, however, as he well knew I would, I succumbed and started a policy with his company.

"You'll never regret this," he said as he got up to go. "After all," he added, "you never know what will happen next week when you're out there," and he gave a seaward jerk of his head.

"Don't be so silly," said Biddie. "In any case, I think it's a complete waste of money. We are just going to have a cup of tea," she went on. "Would you like to have one?"

He was clearly thoroughly astonished at Biddie and excused himself from staying longer by remarking that he had a good deal more work to do. So, quickly, before we changed our minds about the policy, the Black Hawk disappeared down our front path and climbed into his small car. He wasted no time, but started his engine at once and fairly shot away.

The next time he called, I saw him through the sitting-room window, approaching our front door. "Hell. Here's that Old Black Hawk of an insurance man again," I muttered.

"Do come in," said Biddie sweetly.

"So sorry to trouble you," he said.

"Not at all," I replied. "Have a cup of tea." And this time he accepted. He tried to persuade me to increase my policy, but I would not play and he left shortly afterwards with a promise to call again. He did call on several occasions, and on the last visit of all did us a very good turn.

During the first week of February the thaw, followed by some heavy rain, had flooded the valley at the back of our house. The water was still rising and it looked very much as though our bathroom on the ground floor at the back of the house would be flooded. On the seventh of February the wireless gave out "South-east winds increasing to gale force." By three o'clock that same afternoon a full gale was blowing straight into Portmellon. To make matters

worse, it was a sixteen feet eight inch spring tide. By five
o'clock the wind was thundering up the valley and driving
a solid curtain of spray whipped from the crests of the ranks
of oncoming seas that piled into our cove.

We were having our tea when Percy Mitchell came over
with one of his men.

"You're for it tonight," he said. "I'm going to shore you
up," and he proceeded to place a great baulk of timber up
against our front door. He looked at our shutters and shook
his head.

"Think you'll be all right?" he said.

"Oh, yes. I'm sure we shall, Percy," I said, and with
another of his slow and charming smiles he left us.

Around five o'clock some solid spray began to hit the
house, yet there was still two hours to go before high water.
Half an hour later we heard the first dull thud as a sea hit
the wall, followed almost immediately by spray drumming
against our wooden shutters. We ate our supper round the
fire, which hissed indignantly as sea water found its way
down the chimney.

Suddenly, without a word of warning, all the lights went out. We learnt afterwards that some flying seaweed had short-circuited the wires. Fortunately, I had a hurricane lamp, which I lit after a good deal of groping around in the dark for matches and paraffin. By now the fire was completely out and a stream of sea water was leading out of the grate and on to the carpet, which we promptly rolled back. There was no stopping this stream, for it was impossible to block up the chimney. So we worked with brooms and for twenty minutes tried to guide the water through our large downstairs room and out through the back door.

"There's a lot coming under the front room door now," Biddie called out as I guided the chimney stream through the back door.

"Well, it won't be long before there's water coming in here as well," I called back, for to my consternation I saw the flood-water was no more than a yard from our back-door.

By seven o'clock the house was shaking alarmingly to the explosive thuds of the seas. We decided to have a look at the first floor and see how things were going up there, so we climbed the stairs and went into the front bedroom. I was amazed to find the windows still intact. I could see nothing outside, for the pane was constantly covered by sea water.

"I'm going to open the window," I told Biddie. It was a sash window and came down with a rush. At once I was hit in the face by a stinging sheet of spray. But I was determined to see what was happening, so in the brief interval of time before the next wave hit the sea wall I took in all that was going on outside. I heard the next thud of solid water hit the outer wall and instinctively slammed up the window, but not a moment too soon, for the pane was at once washed by what seemed solid water.

What I had seen in those few seconds showed me how serious the storm was. The road itself was full of swirling water which would have covered a car. Immediately below me the sea licked hungrily at our very front door. I thought, though I could not be sure, that I had seen a breach in the sea wall.

There was nothing we could do, so we decided to go to bed. About five o'clock the following morning I became aware of two noises. The first and unmistakable noise was the sound of cascading water pouring down on to the corrugated iron roof of the bathroom below us. The second was a kind of tapping noise, which I could hear only at intervals and with difficulty, for the storm seemed to be, if anything, worse than on the previous night. Our very bed shook, as if in sympathy with the house, against the cruel and prolonged onslaught that it was being forced to undergo. So we lay and listened to the storm and waited for daylight.

At seven we got up and looked out of our back window. The floods in the valley seemed to have risen. We went downstairs and found the ground floor awash, with tar and pieces of seaweed scattered around. I put on my sea boots and Biddie her Wellingtons. I opened the door which led into the porch. At once the sea poured into our sitting-room, and not surprisingly, for the front door that Percy Mitchell had shored up for us had been completely removed and water now sloshed in and out of the porch right up against our sitting-room door. A barrel three-quarters full of potatoes had stood in the porch, but now there was not a sign of a barrel or a single potato. As I stood in the porch the sea swirled in up to my knees. Again there was nothing to be done until the tide dropped. Since there was no electricity we were unable to make a hot drink.

In the back part of the house we found our bath afloat and a foot of water around the lavatory. A storm at the front, floods at the back and no electricity gave us food for thought, if not for stomachs. We had a hurried meal of what we could find and then I waded out, climbed up on to a roof, helped up Biddie, and together we dropped over into Ted Doust's flooded back garden. We had left Kim in our kitchen, much to his disgust.

We waded up to Ted's back door, which was open. A light burned in his kitchen.

In the passage we found Ted in ordinary shoes with his flannel trousers rolled up to his calves, dejectedly sweeping the water through the narrow passage out through his back door.

"I've been banging on the wall since four o'clock," he said. "What the hell have you been doing? Sleeping?"

"That must have been the tapping noise I heard," I replied innocently.

"Well, I've bloody nearly made a hole in the wall banging with a mallet," he growled.

Apparently they had suffered even worse than we had, although miraculously their electricity still worked. Their front door had almost collapsed the previous night but early that morning it had been knocked open and the sea had come in with a vengeance. Some of their upstairs windows were smashed and water poured through the ceilings of all the rooms. We went into the kitchen and I felt warm drops drip from off the electric light bulb on to my forehead. It crossed my mind that we all stood a fair chance of being electrocuted.

His daughter Jo was inside the kitchen with the two terriers, who were lying shivering in a chair. She gave us a cheerful welcome, though it was clear she had not had much sleep during the night.

As I looked around the room it seemed impossible that the whole house had been decorated from top to bottom less than five weeks ago.

"Are the other rooms like this?" I enquired.

"All as bad," she said with a nod of her head.

Ted still stood in the kitchen doorway, which led on to the passage, sweeping the water on its way. After a while he came into the room with a groan and sat down on a damp chair.

"Bring me a dry pair of socks, wench," he snapped at his daughter, and somehow she managed to find him a pair.

With many grunts as he put on his socks and mumbled imprecations against the house and the weather, he told us that he would leave for a week or two, as he could stand no more of this kind of thing.

"I'd never have bought the bloody place if I had known this was going to happen," he mumbled.

"Well, dear," said his daughter, in an attempt to cheer him up, "it will be lovely here in the summer." But nothing we could say or do would brighten his mood.

By nine o'clock the tide had dropped sufficiently for us to go out and survey the damage. The sea wall had been breached and parts of the wall fronting our four houses had been knocked down. Seaweed and pieces of wood were scattered all over the place. Sea birds had been driven ashore and were now resting, battered and bewildered. We picked up one of these creatures, a puffin, and carried him inside. We put him in our flooded bathroom. Kim sniffed at him curiously, but the sea bird, in all appearance a perfect miniature penguin, stood quite still, taking not the slightest notice of the dog. We kept the puffin with us for a day and then we took him down to the sea edge and launched him. He swam away quite happily after his rest, but we could find nothing that interested him in the way of food.

Peter Husband came over to see if he could help, and later Willie Rollins and others walked over from Mevagissey to examine the damage. Several people offered us a bed for the week-end, as the wind was still in the same quarter and the sea very wild.

Percy Mitchell put back our front door and somebody else mended the broken panes of glass in the porch. Another pane had been smashed in one of our top-room windows. We lit a great fire and tried to dry the place out as best we could.

Willie Rollins came over again in the afternoon and had tea with us. I was outside when he arrived and together we examined the storm damage.

"Must have been a bad night," he said as we leant

against the sea wall and looked down the cove at the low, incoming tide. We watched as flashes of bright sunlight momentarily pierced the grey scudding clouds. For a brief interval the torn and scarred surface of the sea would smile in acknowledgment. But then, as though such a shining display was out of keeping with the occasion, the brilliance of the moment would disappear and all would be as before, sombre and wild.

Willie was clearly fascinated by our experiences of the storm and asked many questions, chuckling to himself a good deal. When he got up to leave he took from his wallet a photograph of himself which he presented to us and which we were delighted to have.

Outside I saw him glance quickly at the sky. "The wind's gone back a bit," he observed, "but there's still a lot of sea out there." I watched him as he walked slowly and thoughtfully up the hill towards Mevagissey.

It took three days for the seas to moderate and the winds to lessen. On one of these nights a car attempted to pass Portmellon well before high tide. But the driver mistimed the seas and his car was pushed sideways off the road and on to some shingle. They banged frantically on our front door and we took them in, wet and rather depressed. Not until four hours later could we first examine their Morris. The wheels were almost buried, but the tide had gone back sufficiently for me to get the jeep out and wrench the car out of the deep shingle. Eventually, after we had towed them for some distance, their car fired and started.

One day, when the wind and sea had lessened sufficiently to allow the boats to begin fishing again, I had a long talk with Edgar Husband and Winston Barron about the coming summer months.

"You'm run the red lips this summer," said Edgar with characteristic directness, "and you'll make a good deal more money doing that than spiltering."

Running the red lips was the fishermen's expression for taking visitors out fishing, or just cruising round the bay.

157

I did not look forward to another season of spiltering and the more I thought about taking out visitors, the more the idea appealed to me. However, I had plenty of time to decide; it would be a good many weeks before any visitors really began to appear. But the idea seemed a sound one and it set me thinking. In actual fact everything panned out most satisfactorily, for Sam announced that at the end of netting season he was going to join George Furze, and George Allen had decided his future by buying himself a small motor boat in which to take out visitors. I was sorry to lose Sam and George, but it saved me the job of telling them that I was contemplating running pleasure trips. They had both made their decisions independently. It did not depress me that I was now faced with the prospect of working on my own during the coming summer. In fact, I was looking forward to it all, for now I was confident, I knew the coast and had some idea about what to do when the engines proved awkward. The only slightly dark cloud on our horizon was the knowledge that at the end of May we would once again have to find somewhere new to live. But that was three months distant and we had a feeling that the fishermen would again help us to find a place. And we were right.

CHAPTER TEN

There's a Dog in the Sky

ONE Sunday evening Peter Husband came over full of excitement.

"Plenty of gannets in the bay," he announced in his usual breezy manner.

"Are you going out tonight?" I asked him.

"Bit too late now," he replied, "but some of the boats have gone out."

Fishing on Sunday was, on the whole, avoided, but there were some boats which would go to sea, particularly if there were any signs of fish. The fishermen of Mevagissey treated Sunday as a special day, a day to go to church, to walk the quay in their Sunday best and enjoy their hot Sunday lunch. Fishermen are conservative in mind and habit.

They are also superstitious and would never put their gear aboard a boat, nor start a season of netting or lining, on a Friday. One never mentioned the word rabbits, and if a clergyman were to hover around a boat, let alone come aboard, the chances were that the owner would refuse to put to sea on that particular day. If somebody should make an unguarded remark the crew would at once touch cold iron—for this was the seaman's equivalent of the landlubber's way of touching wood.

On Monday morning we learnt that the few boats that had gone out the previous evening had all had respectable catches. This was exciting news, and we fuelled the *Coral* and took her out to the outer harbour, where we moored her. That night we caught seventy stone of pilchards and finished work at five in the morning. Each night of that week we caught fish and by Thursday morning we had netted 286 stone of pilchards. This was our best week, but I think we were all secretly glad that the following night would mark the end of the week. The hours had been long and the work hard, but I had by this time learnt to forget the tedious, back-breaking hours that lay ahead, and concentrate physically on the job of unmeshing hundreds of pilchards, at the same time remaining mentally detached and far from the actual job. Gradually, as the bottom half of the fish-berth grew full, we would find ourselves standing up to our knees in pilchards. It was as though our sea-boots were wrapped in hot blankets, for the fish exuded a very real warmth.

The shoals of pilchards had been swimming northwards, and on Friday morning, after we had unloaded our fish, Sam, George and I chatted about the coming night. We agreed that we ought to start no later than three-thirty in the afternoon, for the previous night we had been as far as Polperro, and if the fish were still on the move to the north we should probably have to go as far as the Rame. This meant motoring about twenty-seven miles to our destination, and, even provided the weather was fine, it could take the best part of four and a half hours. Shortly afterwards, George and Sam left, and as I walked along the quay I heard a shout from above me. Looking up, I saw Edgar and Peter.

"Going out tonight?" they called down at me from their open windows, which faced directly over the harbour.

"Yes," I replied.

"There's a bit of a dog in the sky," Peter shouted down at me.

"Bit of a what?" and I looked up at them, wondering what new practical joke they had in mind.

"A dog in the sky," said Edgar. "Come up here and I'll show you."

"Look," he said when I stood by his side looking out over the harbour. "See that outer ring round the sun? Well, at the same distance outside that ring there's a spot. We call that a dog or a gulch."

I looked, and sure enough, there was a spot, though I couldn't see that it really resembled a dog. I had heard the fishermen on several occasions remark that there was a bit of a dog in the sky, but till now I had never found out to what they were referring. I asked Edgar what it meant and his answer was short and to the point:

"Bad weather."

I looked again at the sky and the sun. The latter was watery and there was a general haze about, with here and there a few high wisps of white cloud. There was a chill in the air and the wind moaned softly down from the north.

"What's the wireless giving?" I asked.

"It wasn't a good forecast this morning," said Peter. "The wind's gone round to the north, by tonight it'll be easterly."

"It's a long way to the Rame, old boy," said Edgar. "You want to watch your step if you're going up there tonight. If the fish are there, run 'em in, and don't leave your nets in the water too long."

I went home feeling thoughtful. Biddie had been keen to come with us tonight, but after what Edgar and Peter had said I thought it wiser that she should stop behind. At three o'clock I had a cup of tea.

"I think we shall probably be at it all night," I told Biddie as I climbed into the jeep. I looked at her as she stood and waved goodbye. She looked the very picture of health and there was no doubt that she loved the life. I was glad she had Kim as a companion while I was away. Sometimes when we had been working all night she would, unbeknown to me, walk over in the early hours of the morning and watch us as we stood hauling the net over the roller, shaking out the fish. She always liked when possible to stand on the cliff and watch the boats returning from a day on the water. She would tell me later that she could recognise the *Coral* when she was still far out at sea. Then, as the boats approached the harbour, circled by sea-gulls, she would assure me that the prettiest of them all was the *Coral*, with her distinctive turquoise sides, topped by her black strake, her fine uplifted bows pushing the water out of her path as though eager to be home.

I waved goodbye to her and set off in the jeep. On the way I picked up Peter Husband and together we drove into Mevagissey, where I parked the jeep in the south corner of the inner harbour. Most of the crews were down and several engines had already been started.

"See you up at the Rame," called Peter with a laugh as I went down the steps and into the *Babs*, where Sam and George were already waiting. I started up both engines while Sam unshipped the legs and George let go our moorings. In no time we were under way and before we had left the outer harbour I had both engines going full ahead. There were four boats ahead of us, all going north. We settled down to chase them. Already there was an easterly lop, for, just as Peter and Edgar had forecast, the wind had gone round to the east, though as yet it wasn't very strong. The blue sky of the morning had now given place to a grey and overcast ceiling—all the signs of bad weather.

"There was a bit of a dog in the sky this morning, George," I called to him, with a nonchalant air.

"I saw it, me old dear," he said. "Be all right as long as it holds off long enough," he added as he deftly rolled himself a cigarette. Up in the bows Sam too was in the process of rolling himself a cigarette. He took much longer than George, nipping off the odd strands of tobacco and carefully replacing them in his tin. Each of us settled down into a comfortable position and retired within his own thoughts. Astern of us fourteen boats were following, strung out in a long line. I bent down and opened up the Thornycroft to its full extent; glancing over the side I checked the two exhausts. I tested the navigation lights and the engine-room light. All were in good working order. Finally, though still tending the wheel, I pumped the *Coral* dry, a feat made possible by the fact that the pump was alongside the wheel. The last few hideous sucking noises of the pump, which

162

announced that the boat was dry, always produced a frightful stench from the bilges, which were, apart from oil and sludge, full of pilchard scales and the odd rotting fish. After three hours we were abeam of Looe Island, and we were all secretly thankful that the wind had not freshened overmuch. It was growing dark. Some seven miles ahead of us lay the Rame, with Plymouth just round the corner. Fine on our starboard bow the intermittent flash of the lighthouse pierced the gathering gloom and marked the Eddystone Rocks. There were boats ahead of us, already circling, preparatory to shooting their nets. They would have come from Polperro, Looe and Plymouth.

"Plenty of activity between the Eddystone and the Rame," called Sam. I had a look through my binoculars. I could see the gannets diving, plummeting down, white streaks against the now dark background.

We had been overtaken by a number of the Mevagissey luggers, but we were by no means the last. As we drew near the Rame, we saw a scene that will always remain stamped indelibly on my mind. The wind was rising and the occasional sea was breaking, its white crest racing away into the darkness. All around were the black shapes of the boats, their masthead lights dancing above their mizzens. Thick as the first few heavy drops of rain heralding a downpour, the gannets continued to hurtle down on to this concourse of fishing boats, over which every few seconds shone the steady beam of the Eddystone Lighthouse. Hundreds of gulls circled the boats and deafened our ears with their persistent shrieks, which grew more intense as we began to shoot our nets. By half-past seven they were all out, and we had some food and a hot drink. We were hemmed in by boats and I was surprised that some of the nets didn't foul one another.

George went forward and began to pull in a corbal strop. We all looked over the side. Before the first corbal strop was in, it was clear that there were many fish in our nets. I looked at the nearest boats ; their fishing lights were on and I could see the figures of the crew, dark shapes as they pulled their

163

nets under their fishing lights. If they were working, then it
was high time we began; so although the nets had been in
the water for less than half an hour, we began to pull them
in. There were plenty of fish in the first net and in the second
and third nets. Gradually they became even more plentiful
and great thick horse mackerel were caught by the gills and
dragged over the roller to fall loosely into the net-room.
They were too big to become fully enmeshed by the net,
and often I leant over the side and grabbed them before they
drifted astern. I suppose the shock of hitting the net had
killed or partially stunned them. The nets grew heavier and
underneath the black waters a solid wall of white fish hung
down. We had come to the last net and a half, and now I
could see for myself how easy it would be to leave the nets
in the water just that little bit too long, until the weight of
the fish carried the net up and down, and gear and catch were
lost. We had to pull harder than ever before. Already the
headrope and some of our corbal stops were bobbing under
the water, pulled down by the sheer weight of fish. No longer
was it a question of my pulling the headrope and George
the leech, with Sam pulling the after-part. Instead, we all
three gathered great armfuls of shining white net. "White

with fish" I had so often heard the fishermen say; and now here we were pulling it aboard, in just such quantities, each of us sweating and silent with exertion, this wild and black March night.

At last it was finished and the nets were all aboard. I found my legs and arms were trembling and I leant for a moment on the engine-room coaming, before starting the Kelvin. George came aft and pumped her out. I switched on the engine-room light. There was a lot of water in the boat. The deck-board covering the Kelvin's propeller shaft was almost awash.

"Pump hard, George," I called out to him. "We've a hell of a lot of water aboard." Gradually the water in the engine-room grew less and I started the Kelvin. Meanwhile, Sam had secured the mizzen.

It was raining and the wind was on our port side, coming straight in from the east, as Peter had said it would. The *Coral* was low in the water and much more sluggish in her response to the motion of the sea. I opened up both the engines and we began the long return journey. We filled the fuel tanks, Sam holding the filter while I poured five gallons of paraffin and then five gallons of petrol into the Kelvin's and

Thornycroft's tanks respectively. We decided against attempting to shake out any pilchards on the way home, for the motion of the boat was too severe. Sam remained up in the bows while George and I took it in turns steering the *Coral*. During my off spells I pumped her out and then stood in the engine-room, feeling the warmth of the engines beneath me.

We slogged on through the night, trying to pick out landmarks through the curtain of rain. Once the *Coral* rolled heavily and nearly dipped her port gunwale. I think she would have shipped a good deal of water had it not been for her seven-inch strake.

We had left the Rame shortly after nine o'clock, and four hours later we picked up Mevagissey Light, shining thinly through the wet night. We had come down with the ebb tide and outside Fowey had found a nasty steep sea, the result of the outgoing tide meeting the incoming easterly seas. But in spite of her heavy load the *Coral* carried us across this turbulent stretch of water and on towards the Black Head and Mevagissey Harbour.

By half-past one we had tied up in the inner harbour, shipped our roller across the net-room and begun to shake out the pilchards. Nine hours later, just on half-past ten that same morning, we had finished and were ready to go home. I climbed into the jeep and drove back to Portmellon. Biddie was out, so I took off my sea-boots and sank like a sack of potatoes into an armchair. I did not attempt to move, but sat relaxed, letting my weariness envelop me, for there was now no longer any need to combat physical exhaustion.

As I sat there, utterly fatigued, my mind seemed to become detached from my body and I was able, clearly and without effort, to look back dispassionately on the night's work.

We had been on our feet for nineteen hours. The *Coral* had covered over fifty miles. From half-past one onwards, we had worked through the early hours of the morning, hauling the heavy net over the roller, flicking, banging, shaking the hundreds of pilchards out of the nets into the fish-berth below. Gradually the grey dawn had revealed the sleeping village, and we had stopped for a few minutes to drink from our thermos flasks. All around us other crews were hard at work, and the noise of the rollers clicking incessantly, as the nets were pulled over them, mingled with the sound of pilchards being slapped against oilskin smocks.

Against this background of noise there had been a constant chatter coming from one of the luggers. It was, of course, the *Pride of the West*, and it had made me smile to think that, no matter how arduous and how long the occasion, Albert and his merry men were still chattering as fast and as hard as ever. Most crews work silently, ruthlessly thrashing the net, till the pilchards fly thick and fast down into the fish pen. But the *Pride of the West* were a law unto themselves and the faster they worked the more they talked.

Towards the end of these eight exhausting hours of shaking out pilchards, Waller had come over several times to see how much longer we were going to be.

"Hurry up, Ken, or you'll not be ready for the kick-off this afternoon," he had remarked quite seriously on his last visit. I hoped that I had managed a smile, but my mind was far too intent on one thing and one thing only : shaking the last pilchard out of the last net. Eventually this moment had arrived and I had gone up with thirty baskets of fish, which were promptly weighed by Horace. We had caught 103 stone of pilchards and 76 stone of mackerel, a total of 179 stone in all. Horace handed me the chit on which was written our catch.

"I couldn't possibly play football today, Horace," I had told him. "I'm whacked, though I hate to disappoint Catherine."

"All right, old man," he said. "I'll tell 'em."

I sat and mused and drifted asleep. I was rudely woken some time later by Kim's wet nose and hot tongue.

"Hello," said Biddie, her face aglow and her hair wind-swept. "We watched you from the top of the hill, but decided not to come down because we didn't want to disturb you." This was typical of her quiet approach and thoughtfulness, which had been such a help to me during these months, and though I have no doubt that at that moment I probably only answered her remark with a grunt, if anything at all, I was in actual fact deeply grateful to her for all her support.

"I'll put the kettle on," she said. "I've never seen so many pilchards as you had aboard. How many stone did you catch?"

"A hundred and seventy-nine," I answered.

It was a good catch for the *Coral*, though Cyril Hunkin, when he had owned the boat, had once carried 400 stone of dogfish in her. The *Coral*, however, would not have carried 400 stone of pilchards with the additional weight of nets. All the boats had done well and several luggers had caught 600 stone. Jim Behennah had unfortunately lost six nets, which had been carried down to the bottom of the sea by sheer weight of fish.

On Monday morning we were paid by J.B. That week we had netted a total of 465 stone of fish, comprising 386 stone of pilchards and 79 stone of mackerel. For the latter we were paid 3s. 3d. a stone; our total week's work was worth £51 8s. 9d. By the time our expenses had been deducted we had just over £48 to share. This sum was divided into five equal shares of £9 12s. 6d.: Sam and George each had one share and I took three, one for the boat, one for the nets and one for myself, giving me £28 17s. 6d. for those five days of pilchard driving.

We carried on fishing during the following weeks, but though we caught some pilchards we never again had such good fishing. On one occasion, when Biddie was aboard, we heard a great shoal of fish breaking the surface. "Sometimes you'll hear them on a calm night," the fishermen had said, "making a noise like running water." Even as we listened, a great black shape rose slowly out of the water, just off our starboard side and with a hiss blew a jet of water into the air. It was a whale, whom the fishermen referred to as the Hog.

All the time the nights were becoming shorter and the weather much finer. On another night a crew shot their nets a short distance off Mevagissey Light; a shark got into their nets and caused a lot of damage. They killed the fish and next morning his twenty-foot carcase lay alongside the quay, grotesque and already beginning to smell.

In the second week of April Ted Doust and his daughter Jo once again took up residence. The old chap was full of foreboding, but determined at any rate to give the summer a go. We now had neighbours on both sides of us. Shortly after the Dousts had returned, Ebi and Noel Lucas took up residence in the house next door. I was out most nights fishing and, apart from a friendly wave to them and a casual good morning, we had seen nothing of them.

However, one lunchtime Ebi appeared at the door with a large dish and I heard Biddie thanking her warmly.

"What on earth have you got there?" I asked her rather crossly as she put the large covered dish on the table.

"Hungarian goulash," she replied. "Ebi wondered if you'd like some."

I must confess I did not particularly like the idea of food suddenly appearing from people one had never really met. I watched as Biddie lifted the top off the large oval dish. Underneath was a magnificent Hungarian goulash, piping hot and beautifully arranged.

Good heavens, I thought. What on earth will happen next? Fortunately, ours was going to be a cold lunch, and we quickly warmed two plates and started to eat this wonderful meal.

Afterwards we went across to return the dish and thank Ebi. Noel Lucas opened the door and asked us in for coffee. His manner was suave and he was immaculately dressed. I learnt later that all his suits—and he had nine with him— were made in Savile Row. Ebi was amused by my fishing smock, which made a splendid contrast to the elegance of Noel. They asked many questions about the fishing, and by the time we had left Noel had decided that he must have a small dinghy with an outboard. They had taken the house for a year and as a side-line were making plastic bags for some of the West End stores. When we got up to leave they asked us for dinner at the end of the week. We accepted with alacrity.

I was down on the quayside the following morning when Winston Barron and Willie Wish came up to me.

"My God," said Willie. "There's a great vessel of a boat just come into the outer harbour. The skipper aboard is asking for you."

"Is she a Brixham trawler?" I asked.

"Why, yes," he said. "Do you know the boat?"

"I think I know the owner," I replied. "I'll go along and see if it's the chap I think it is."

I was right. It was Guy Greville and I was delighted to see him. He wanted to buy something in the village, so we visited the shops before going aboard. Fortunately, we ran into Biddie in the village. We all had a cup of coffee and then went aboard Guy's Brixham trawler. She was indeed a magnificent boat. He had bought her from A. E. W. Mason and she was beautifully fitted out below, with a fine auxiliary diesel engine. He was doing some trawling from Fowey, but finding it skilled and difficult work. He did not know the bottom and he'd lost one or two trawls. But if he was discovering that fishing was hard work and far from lucrative, outwardly he gave no sign. He was still the same person, charming and poker-faced. We watched him as he got under way, managing the boat with only one other hand aboard. I admired him, for it took courage, even if it was perhaps a little unwise, to take on a boat this size. I saw Guy and his family once more over at Fowey, and learnt that he was contemplating buying an old steel steamship and carrying coal up the coast. He was supremely confident about it all, though in actual fact it did not materialise. I never saw Guy again; I believe he went into the mushroom-growing business.

In April Sam left to start fishing with George Furze, so I was back where I had started, fishing the *Coral* with George Allen. For three weeks we continued pilchard-driving and then it was time for George to leave us and start work on his own motor boat.

It was also time for me to start painting the *Coral* again.

But our immediate problem was to find somewhere to live during the coming summer. And here again we were lucky. We had been tipped the wink by a crabber called Henry Johns that one of the cottages on Bodrugan Farm was empty.

"Go and see Kendall, who owns Bodrugan, and he'll probably let you have it for the summer," said Henry.

We wasted no time and the following day Biddie and I went to Bodrugan to see Leo Kendall.

"Yes," he said, looking at us shrewdly though not unkindly. "You can have the cottage for the summer." We thanked him and he gave us the key.

So, one morning at the end of May, we piled everything into the jeep and began our fifth and last move, into Bodrugan Cottage. It was semi-detached and comparatively modern; magnificently situated, perched at the top of Bodrugan hill, overlooking the sea. At night we could see the lights of Portmellon beneath us, while to the north the bright flash of Fowey Light caught the eye.

There were six rooms in the cottage—three up, three down. There was no electricity, no gas and the water had to be pumped from a well. Outside, at the back, was a small rickety wooden contraption, tucked away forlornly amidst the nettles and overshadowed by the branches of a tree. This was supposed to be the lavatory, but the hens had made such a frightful mess that we decided it was out of the question to use it. The kitchen contained an old-fashioned range which I struggled to light. After a while Ivy, from next door, came across and asked if she could be of any help.

171

In no time she had taken over and got our fire to go. But it was soon clear to us that the kitchen range was not going to be the answer to the cooking problem. That afternoon we took the jeep into St Austell and purchased, besides pots and pans and a double bed and mattress, another primus stove and an oven built to be used on it, in which we could cook a joint. We also bought an Elsan and the necessary chemical. On the way back we picked up a large, red carpet, dilapidated though colourful, from Mevagissey.

We lit a fire in the evening and it burned surprisingly well in the high grate. The yellow light of the paraffin lamp gave a warm glow to the small room. Later we climbed the narrow wooden stairs and undressed by the light of a hurricane lamp. Through the open window the warm night air smelt fresh and sweet. Above the water hung a bright, thin crescent moon and away in the distance the intermittent white light of the Eddystone winked and blinked its warning to ships.

CHAPTER ELEVEN

Bodrugan

NEXT door lived the mother and father of Ivy, who had helped us light our stove. We grew fond of the old couple, particularly the old lady, whom we called "Madame Parrot," for it was impossible to understand a word she was saying. The hot weather had lowered the water in the well and she would become furious with the pump, eventually in her anger giving it a kick when no water was forthcoming. We would go to her aid and she would grin with pleasure. The old man, on the other hand, was quite different. I never once heard him speak and we saw him only on certain occasions. These occurred regularly at ten o'clock in the morning when, infinitely slowly, he would set out for the privy, some fifteen yards from their back door.

In the meantime I had begun running long-distance pleasure trips to Fowey, Polperro and St Mawes. Provided the weather was fine, it was both lucrative and easy work. On a good day I found I could easily earn six or seven pounds. But somehow I never enjoyed taking the money from my passengers. The weather was fine, the sea calm, the coastline magnificent and the passengers happy. It didn't seem right that they should have to pay for it all in hard cash. That they thought it was worth the money was clear, for many of them came again.

But we had got to live, and there's no doubt that I earned a great deal more money than ever I would have done had I continued spilter-lining for whiting.

Still the weather continued fine and there were more visitors than ever.

"Plenty of red lips," the fishermen would say as the

visitors strolled along the quayside, or crowded around a long-liner which had just come alongside to offload her catch.

Long-liners work six or seven thousand hooks. They go away about six in the evening and shoot eight or nine pilchard nets in order to catch their bait. On nights when they are unable to catch a sufficient number of pilchards to bait their enormous length of line, they will go alongside the other drifters and see if they can buy their bait from them.

Once the long-liner has sufficient quantity of bait the crew will cut up the pilchards and start baiting the hundreds of hooks. The skipper will take the wheel and head the lugger out to sea, and those who can will sleep in the forecastle. They will go off forty or fifty miles, shoot their line, haul it, clear it of fish and head for home. It is a twenty-four-hour round trip of hard work and precious little rest.

I had just moored the *Coral* one afternoon and was preparing to go ashore, when a lugger came gently alongside the quay. She had been away long-lining and I watched with interest as her crew methodically and quickly went about their work. They seemed completely oblivious of the crowd that had gathered, partly because they were physically very tired; but I noticed as the summer wore on and the village became more and more crowded, that those who were fishing in earnest for their living retained a certain aloof dignity and resignation, for their village as they had known it was in the process of being destroyed under their very eyes. It was no longer easy for the old ones to be sure of finding a seat around the harbour, and if they did find one their view was usually obstructed by the passing crowds and the cars that inched their way along the crowded quays.

Already, although this was only my second summer and destined to be my last as an inhabitant, I could see a difference in the village of Mevagissey. Lofts were being turned into cafés, souvenirs filled the shop-windows, and guesthouse and bed and breakfast signs were displayed everywhere.

Against this shifting background of holiday-makers the fishermen manœuvred their boats, mended their nets, baited their lines and landed their fish. Quietly and patiently they tolerated the invasion, for it meant money. As I sat in the *Coral* and watched the crowds I felt sad that the character of the village was changing so quickly. True, the fishermen who owned toshers would be sure to earn money by running the red lips, provided the weather was fine, but what of the bigger boats? What advantage would the crowded summer months bring to the crews? Their wives could, of course, take in paying guests in their homes, and some of them did, but apart from this there was no advantage. The sad truth was that inshore fishing had become an anachronism and was dying out in Mevagissey, just as it had done in so many other fishing villages.

All that summer I ran pleasure trips, but my heart was not really in the work, for I knew there was no real future for me doing this, unless I was prepared to think in terms of a bigger and faster boat, with a Board of Trade certificate so that I could carry more passengers. That meant charging lower prices and undercutting the other boats. This I would never have done—for the fishermen were our friends and we would have been competing against those who had been so good to us.

One afternoon I was driving back to Bodrugan when I saw Mr Kendall standing outside his cottage in Portmellon. I stopped the jeep and got out in order to talk to him. That short conversation changed the whole course of my life.

"Are you going to try and make a living from the sea for the rest of your life?" he asked me.

"I don't know," I replied truthfully.

"Why don't you try and get up to one of the universities? After all, as an ex-Serviceman you are entitled to a grant. At any rate, I should think about it," he added.

And I did. I thought hard over the week-end and I talked it over with Biddie. It was crystal clear that I was never going to make a fortune at fishing. During the war the fishermen had made a lot of money, though very often under hazardous conditions. To give an idea of the kind of money that had been made, I knew of one fisherman who, on his own, had made a hundred pounds in one week, plummeting for mackerel. But those days were over and to earn a good living at fishing was no longer easy. There were boats that did well, but they had to go out in all weathers and work prodigious hours. One of these boats was the *Ibis*, a fine lugger with diesel engines, owned by the Lakemans. They were a quiet crew, dedicated to their job, all magnificent fishermen. I knew as I talked to them that they were in mind, if not in body, thirty miles out at sea, drawn away from the land as if by a magnet. On a Sunday morning, dressed in their best suits, they looked out of their element as they paced the quayside, waiting for the early hours of Monday morning. The sea was their life and they were a part of it.

If I was to continue a fisherman I must expect to work these long hours and eventually be able to compete with a crew like the *Ibis*. I knew that I would never be able to do this; apart from the fact that I should need much more capital, which I did not possess, I would require a crew. The crew problem was a very real one, for the men aboard the luggers were growing old and the youngsters were not coming into fishing. I, as an outsider, would find this crew problem even more difficult.

The more I considered the matter the more I realised that Mr Kendall was right, and that I should attempt to obtain some qualification. And so, that very week-end, I sat down and wrote several letters to both Oxford and Cambridge, asking if it was possible for me to come up to the University that September. Their replies were prompt and to the point. There was absolutely no chance whatsoever. The universities were already far too full and, much as they all regretted it, they were unable to help. But I did not give up and wrote again and again, until eventually I must have written to most of the colleges at both Oxford and Cambridge. I had tried all the smaller colleges, and now I was left with one or two of the bigger ones.

I knew that Brasenose took a number of Shrewsbury boys, so to Brasenose I applied in a last, forlorn hope. "I am a fisherman," I wrote, "and though I love the life, I find it hard to make ends meet." I thought I had better let them know more about myself, for I felt that if nothing came of this letter, then Oxford and Cambridge were definitely out. So I informed them that I was a married man, had been educated at Shrewsbury School, had played for the School at football, cricket and fives, served five years in the Navy and won the Distinguished Service Cross. I showed the letter to Biddie.

"Do you think it sounds too much of a good thing?" I asked her.

"No," she said. "I don't. Send it off just as it is." And I did.

I found that I was seeing less of the fishermen. They were just as friendly and helpful as ever, but I was now working on my own, and although the trips I ran in the *Coral* up and down the coast were happy occasions, I missed the gruff companionship of George Pearce, the stories of George Allen and the sight of Sam Ingrouille standing tall and resigned to the fact that before him were hundreds of hooks waiting to be cleared and baited up. Above all, I missed that exciting moment when the creeper was in sight and the line itself visible, slanting away to the bottom of the sea. That was the moment we all awaited. Crews, with of course, one exception—the *Pride of the West*—never talk as the first part of the line or net is hauled inboard. It is a moment of intense drama which never palls, for each man knows that on that line or in that net hangs his pounds, shillings and pence. Whether or not there are plenty of fish on the line or in the net, no comments are ever made. It is all closely bound up with the fact that fishermen for generations have known the hardship of toil and poverty and, being naturally superstitious, as are all those who wrest their living from the sea, they will never tempt Providence by an unguarded word of enthusiasm or disappointment, let alone a prediction of what might or might not be on the line or in the net.

My pounds, shillings and pence now lay sprawled over the *Coral's* decks. They were nice people, easy to catch, easy to handle and easy to off-load, and they made me good money. But I missed the excitement of those vague green shapes that slanted away into the dark water. They were not so certain and obvious as those on the *Coral's* decks, nor were they so lucrative, but I preferred them all the same. I also knew in my heart of hearts that I should never see them again as one trying to earn a living as a fisherman.

Going into Mevagissey one morning, I stopped the postman and asked him if he had any letters for us. There was one from the Principal of Brasenose College, W. T. S. Stallybrass. He wrote:

Dear Sir,
    I am obliged to you for your letter of the 28th of May. The College is, of course, extraordinarily over-full and admission is very highly competitive, but if you would

care to come up for our College Entrance Examination on July 1st and 2nd, we should be very pleased to examine you. Would you please complete the enclosed College Entry Form if you wish to come up. I do not, of course, at present know whether you are exempt from Responsions.

Mevagissey brings up happy memories to me.

Yours sincerely,

W. T. S. Stallybrass.

I was rather intrigued by the second and third words of his last sentence, and wondered whether he had been out fishing and suffered from the motion of the boat. At any rate, this was the most hopeful reply to date. The door had not been politely but firmly shut in my face. However, the prospect of a College Entrance Examination appalled me. My academic career had been very average. It was only at the second attempt that I had attained the necessary number of credits in the School Certificate for matriculation, though I found later that this did exempt me from Responsions. But what on earth, I wondered, would I have to do for this College Entrance Examination? However, there was hope, so I wrote back at once to W. T. S. Stallybrass, saying that I would very much like to sit the College Entrance Examination, but that I feared the results would be terrible. "I have not sat an examination for eight years, apart from one on gunnery, in which I scored five out of a hundred," I wrote.

Four days later I heard again from the Principal:

Dear Mr Shearwood,

Thank you for your letter of the 2nd of June. You should not worry too much about the Entrance Examination. Allowances will be made for the fact that it is a long time since you have done that sort of work.

Yours sincerely,

W. T. S. Stallybrass.

179

I also heard from the Ministry of Education, to whom I had previously written, asking whether I would be entitled to receive a grant. Their reply was, I thought, rather ominous. After quoting from the Government pamphlet P.L. 120, they wanted to know why I wished to discontinue my career as an architect at Liverpool University and study for a History Degree. They ended up by explaining that they could do nothing until they had received definite confirmation that I had been accepted by a university.

Things were moving, but my chances of getting into Oxford still appeared very remote.

The following week my old Commanding Officer, Peter Bull, came down to stay with us. He was fascinated and enchanted by Bodrugan Cottage. His bedroom was tiny, and without raising himself from his pillow he could look straight out to sea.

Before supper that evening we all had a swim and then sat down to a large meal of crab. We sat around an old gate-legged oak table, its fine surface mellow with age. For chairs we used three empty five-gallon petrol drums and two new upturned fish-boxes. They were not particularly comfortable, but perfectly adequate.

The following morning we were all awoken by Peter with a cup of tea.

"Had a little trouble with the primus," he announced cheerfully. "I filled it up with methylated spirits instead of paraffin."

By the morning's post I heard again from Brasenose College, enclosing the time-table of their entrance examination. "We should naturally expect you to take a General Paper, a History Paper and French Unseen Translation," they wrote. They concluded by saying that they would be obliged if I would let them know what period of History I was going to offer and whether it was English or European, or both. The period should cover not less than a hundred years.

After a hurried consultation, it was unanimously decided that the Tudors and the Stuarts were the answer.

Halfway through June I began to think about my Entrance Examination for Brasenose. I had heard from some source or other that Mrs Clarke, the wife of the Post-master, was interested in history.

"Yes, my dear," she said when I called on her. "I've always loved the subject, but I've only got a small book giving a general outline. Take it by all means."

I thanked her and went away with the book, which covered two thousand odd years of history in some two hundred and fifty pages. It did not take me long to read the period on which I was to be examined. In a few pages the author had covered the lives of Henry VIII and Elizabeth; the unfortunate Henry VII, Edward VI and Mary had a page between the lot of them.

I browsed through the book, lying on the *Coral's* warm deck while my passengers were ashore.

"Have a good day?" Biddie would ask when I got back in the evening. "Know all about the Dissolution of the Monasteries?" Peter would enquire.

At the end of June we set off for Evesham, where I left Biddie and Kim at her old home while I went on to Oxford. I took with me sufficient for two nights and, of course, my little brown history book, which I looked at the night before the examinations.

On 1 July I sat three papers. The examination room was full of candidates and they all looked most earnest young men. In the morning I wrote a French Unseen Translation. I knew the meaning of very few of the words and had to guess most of it. From ten-thirty onwards I wrote a General Paper. Here I was faced by a number of subjects of which I was required to write on four. I remember clearly one of the questions which I attempted: "Faithful study of the higher arts softens the character and preserves us from savagery. Discuss this view of the moral and social value of art." What I wrote I cannot imagine, but I do remember distinctly thinking as I sat there how much the fishermen would have laughed had they seen me at that moment attempting to answer this question. In the afternoon I wrote a history paper. I scarcely covered two pages, for my little brown history book was found sadly wanting. I searched feverishly for a question about Wolsey. I found one, "Do you consider that Wolsey played a brilliant but essentially futile part on the European stage?" It didn't really seem to help very much. I eventually handed in my paper well before time. That evening I wandered around Oxford and looked at the lovely old buildings. I visited the Parks, where the University played cricket. I caught a bus which took me over Magdalen Bridge, along Iffley Road and dropped me outside the University football ground. I should really have been worrying about my papers, for I knew they would far from satisfy the examiners. But somehow it didn't seem to matter.

Next morning we were all interviewed. When my turn came I rather looked forward to seeing what they were all like. I knocked on the door and walked into a gracious room, where a group of Dons sat round a long table, at the head of which sat Dr Stallybrass. I got the impression of a heavily built man with a kind and wise face.

"Sit down please, Mr Shearwood," he said, and I found myself sitting in the midst of them.

"You were in the Navy?" he asked me.

"Yes, sir."

"You won the Distinguished Service Cross?"

"Yes, sir."

"And since the war you've been fishing for your living?"

"I have, sir."

There was a pause and Dr Stallybrass gave a cough.

"What flies have you been using?" I heard a voice ask me from the other end of the table, and I could feel them all looking at me.

"We didn't use flies at all. I have been inshore fishing in Cornwall as a profession."

Then, for the next ten minutes, perhaps longer, I answered their questions and thoroughly enjoyed telling them about it.

"Thank you, Mr Shearwood," said Dr Stallybrass, and I rose to leave.

"We will let you know the result in the course of the next few days," he said. I thanked him and left the room in a happy frame of mind.

We motored straight back to Cornwall, and the following afternoon I took some passengers to Fowey.

Three days later I came back from an all-day trip to Polperro. It had been a hot day and I could still feel the glow of the sun on my face and arms as I drove back to Bodrugan Cottage. Biddie was in the porch.

"There's a letter from Oxford," she said.

"Is there? Now we'll know one way or the other."

I opened it immediately.

Dear Mr Shearwood,
    I have much pleasure in informing you . . .

I read no further.

"It's all right," I said. "They've accepted me."

It was wonderful news and we were both very excited. But gradually the prospect that we were to leave Mevagissey and the fishermen and go back and live inland saddened us.

"There's always the holidays," I told Biddie. "We shan't lose touch with them."

That evening we went down to Mevagissey and told Willie Rollins. I could see he was upset that we were going, but he brightened up when I slipped a packet of Woodbines into his hand.

"We shall come back, Willie, as much as we can, and we've not gone yet."

Later on we met Willie Wish. Somehow the word had already got round that we were leaving. He came rolling towards us, peering up at us from under the peak of his cap.

"Well, Missus," he said, courteously addressing Biddie

first, "so he's got into Oxford University. Well I'm very pleased for both your sakes."

I thanked him. "I'm afraid I shall have to sell the *Coral*," I added regretfully.

"Never mind, old man," he said. "What we've got to do is find a buyer. You leave that to us. We'll find a Joe."

In July Nicholas Phipps joined us in Bodrugan Cottage. He and Peter had been at Winchester together and, being actors, had much in common. I wondered now, as I looked at Nick's tall and elegant figure, how he would like the cottage and still more his camp-bed, not to mention the Elsan and the primus stove. He had survived his first night, though I suspect the rows of bottles of pills and medicines that surrounded the camp-bed had much to do with it.

Still the sun shone and in no time July and nearly all of August had slipped away. I was now beginning to worry a little, for I had received no offer for the *Coral*.

I had tried advertising her in the paper, but without result. It was clear I was going to lose about three hundred pounds, unless the fishermen could find me a Joe who would be prepared through inexperience to pay the sum that I gave for the *Coral*. But Willie Wish did not seem particularly concerned.

"We'll find you a Joe, old man," he said when I talked to him about the subject. And he did.

One day in the last week of August I had come home after an all-day trip to Polperro. I was sitting in our rocking-chair, my eyes closed, pushing the chair gently backwards and forwards with my stockinged feet, when I was suddenly aroused by a knock on the door.

I opened it and there was Willie Wish.

"Come in, Willie," I said, "and have a cup of tea."

"No, old man, I'm not staying. I'm going straight back. I came up to tell you I've found a Joe. Be down on the quay tomorrow morning at half-past nine and ask £720 for her. You'll get it."

I tried to persuade him to come in, and when he wouldn't

I said that I would run him back to Mevagissey, for it was a long and hilly walk for an old man. But it was no use. Willie insisted on walking and he was one of those people whose word was final. I was most touched and grateful that he should have walked all the way over from Mevagissey to tell me this piece of news.

"Don't forget, be down at nine-thirty sharp and £720's the price," he called to me.

I went back into Bodrugan Cottage. It looked as though the time had come when we were to part with the *Coral*.

"It's very sad," said Biddie when I told her the news.

The following morning I was down at the quay well before the appointed time. Promptly at half-past nine Willie Wish appeared with three men. One was obviously a business man; the other two were fishermen. I took them all aboard the *Coral* and started up her engines. The business man had a talk with his two fishermen and we all eventually went ashore.

"Well," said the business man, "what are you asking for her?"

"£700," I answered. I don't know why I did not say £720, as Willie had instructed me. Perhaps I felt the *Coral* owed me nothing.

"I'll give you £680," he said.

"That's all right," I told him, and he wrote me out a cheque for £680.

His two men, who were going to fish the boat for him, were to take the *Coral* straight away down to Mousehole. I shook hands with the business man and then took a long, last look at the *Coral* as she lay at her moorings. Her fine, blunt, uplifted bow seemed to look me straight in the face as though I had deserted her, and as I turned and walked away I felt distinctly sad, for the *Coral* was now no longer ours.

At the end of the quay I met Willie Wish.

"All right, old man?" he enquired.

"Yes," I replied. "I sold her for £680."

"Did you ask £720?"

"No," I admitted.

185

"You'm damned old fool," said Willie Wish. "If you'd stuck out, you'd have got your price. Still I'm very glad for your sake you've sold her."

I thanked him as warmly as I could for all he'd done, and then told him that I wanted him to have forty pounds as he'd saved me a good three hundred, and probably even more.

"Do take it, Willie," I said quietly, but nothing I could say or do would make him accept anything. I glanced once again at the *Coral* and saw that they were already casting off her moorings preparatory to leaving for Mousehole. I climbed into the jeep and drove slowly and thoughtfully back to Bodrugan Cottage.

"Come on," I said to Biddie. "Let's go to the Dodman and look at the *Coral* for the last time." We took the jeep to the top of Hemmick Bay and then walked to the Dodman.

It was a wild and wonderful day. The sea lay blue beneath us; white horses whipped up by the wind danced in the sunlight. While Kim rushed around in the deep bracken we waited for the *Coral*. We waited for over an hour, but she never came. She may have put back into Mevagissey or she may have had engine trouble. I never found out what happened and I never enquired. There we stood on that bright, windy day, at the top of that great cliff, and waited for the *Coral*, but she never came. She had gone from our lives and we never saw her again.

We decided that we would have to leave at the end of the second week of September. There was a week to go. Willie Rollins helped me dispose of my nets and my lines. My smocks, seaboots, oilskins, gaffs, creepers, grapnels, Aldis lamp and various other small items I gave away.

I spent the last week talking to the fishermen and saying goodbye to our friends. We were both deeply sorry to be going. Not for a moment did either of us regret those nineteen months. I had only tasted a fisherman's life, but it had been sufficient to show me that it was a life full of a simple dignity that required both a philosophy and a sense of humour. They were warm and generous people and I knew how much we would miss them.

Our last night in Bodrugan Cottage was a strange one. Everything had been packed up and what little furniture we possessed had been stored in a room in Bodrugan Farmhouse. All that remained were our suitcases and pots and pans and primus stoves, which stood on the stone floor in the kitchen. We climbed the steep, narrow flight of wooden stairs. The night was peaceful and beautiful, and we stood at our window and looked for the last time at Fowey Light as it winked at us across seven miles of dark water. Some boats were out pilchard-driving. As I watched the yellow pinpoints of their mast-head lamps flickering in the darkness, I remembered vividly that first night out in the *Coral*, till I could feel again the weight of the headrope, smell the tar in the nets, hear the shriek of the gulls and see the shimmering fish in the tracery of mesh. Suddenly the headlights of a passing car momentarily dazzled us as it reached the top of Bodrugan Hill and jerked me back to reality.

Around midnight I gradually became conscious of strange noises down below. I lay and listened, and there was no doubt that something was happening. Kim was wide awake; he always slept at the foot of our bed. He growled uncomfortably. There was silence for a while and then again came a sound of footsteps and shuffling, and I could hear the pots and pans clanking around as though they were being moved. My first thought was that perhaps Madame Parrot was up and about next door. I listened carefully, but there was no doubt whatsoever that the noises came from our two rooms down below.

"What's happening down there?" Biddie asked me.

"I don't know," I replied. "And I'm not going down to find out. We'll leave well alone."

The noises continued for the next hour, and Kim was restless and whimpered occasionally. Gradually we fell asleep.

Just before first light Biddie awoke to the sound of

footsteps coming slowly up the stairs. For a moment she thought I had been down below and was coming back. But as she became fully alert she realised to her alarm that I was by her side. Now very much awake she heard the footsteps reach the top of the stairs and then slowly approach our door. To her great relief they shuffled past and went on into Peter's empty room next door. Kim had stood up and made strange half-whining, half-growling noises which awoke me. Biddie told me what she had just heard, and we lay and listened as the first light of dawn stole into the room. But we heard nothing more. We dozed off again and awoke to bright sunshine.

Intrigued, we dressed quickly and pushed Kim out of the room first. We made a quick inspection of the other two rooms upstairs and then went below. Nothing seemed to have been disturbed. We imagined the pots and pans might have been moved around, but this was not the case. There was no sign of any disturbance whatsoever. We thought of the possibility of rats. But we had never seen any and there were no holes by which they could have entered. Nor, on reflection, could they have possibly made the noises that we had heard that night.

After breakfast we went over to say goodbye to Madame Parrot.

"Were either of you up in the night?" we asked her.

She shook her head vigorously.

"Did you hear any noises?" Again she shook her head. I filled her bucket for the last time and we said goodbye to her. There were tears in the old lady's eyes.

Soon after eight we began to pack up the jeep. Just as we had started who should arrive but the Old Black Hawk.

"Good gracious," I said. "You are just in time to give us a hand."

In no time his arms were full as he carried innumerable objects from the cottage to the jeep. At last we were all packed in.

"I heard you were going and I wanted to catch you

before you left," said the insurance man. "Now what about increasing the policy?"

"One good turn deserves another. Yes, of course, I'll increase it, but only by a very little," I told him.

Ivy and her husband had arrived to say goodbye. Madame Parrot was there, and I could see the old man looking through the window. So, with a wave from them all, including the insurance man, we started the jeep and drove slowly away from Bodrugan Cottage. At the top of Polkirt Hill we paused and looked down once again at the inner and outer harbour. Yet another day had begun.

Below me I could see the *Margaret* and the *Ibis*, the *Pride of the West*, the *White Heather* and the *Little Pearl*. They were all there. Except the *Coral*. She had gone.

I let in the clutch of the jeep and plunged down Polkirt Hill. I felt Kim's heavy head rest on my shoulder as we drove through the village of Mevagissey and away, up and over the hill towards new fishing grounds at some place called Oxford.

Lightning Source UK Ltd.
Milton Keynes UK
23 April 2010

153255UK00001B/17/P